A Parents' Guide
to Child Safety

A
Parents'
Guide to
Child
Safety

Vincent J. Fontana, M.D., F. A. A. P.

Thomas Y. Crowell Company
NEW YORK • ESTABLISHED 1834

Illustrations by Henry Roth

Designed by Ingrid Beckman

Manufactured in the United States of America

ISBN 0-690-00081-2

1   2   3   4   5   6   7   8   9   10

Library of Congress Cataloging in Publication Data

Fontana, Vincent J.
    A parent's guide to child safety.

    1. Children—Wounds and injuries.   2.   Children's accidents.
I. Title. [DNLM: 1. Accident prevention—In infancy and
childhood. 2. Accidents, Home—In infancy and childhood.
3. Accidents, Home—Prevention and control. WA288 F679p
1973]
RD93.5.C4F64   614.8'53   73-10185
ISBN 0-690-00081-2

*To Sister Margaretta Maria Brock, R.N.,
whose entire life has been dedicated to
the care of children*

Introduction

John P. McCann, M.D.
Medical Director
Life Extension Institute

Growing up is a risky business. Each day children face risks—risks of accidents, illness, injury, disability, and even death. Whether children live, die, or are disabled often lies squarely on the shoulders of adults. Granted that children must face risks all the time, this does not mean we cannot do something about them; we can and must. While any child may be afflicted or even killed by any of hundreds of health hazards at each point in his life, there are only a few that constitute major threats. In childhood, these are principally accidents and poisonings. If these major hazards are identified and quantified, a list of specific threats can be isolated. These, of course, will be different for given age brackets, home situations, and general environmental conditions and whether the child is a boy or girl. Once the risks are out in the open, however, it is possible to develop a plan to reduce or eliminate them. Such is the purpose of Dr. Fontana's book, *A Parents' Guide to Child Safety*.

The approach often referred to as "health hazard appraisal" forms the matrix for the practice of prospective medicine, the newest branch of the health care field. Drs.

Robbins and Hall of Methodist Hospital in Indianapolis, Indiana, utilize this method in identifying health hazards for all age groups. The only difference for the adult group is that, as we grow older, accidents gradually assume a less dominant role and are replaced by diseases of the heart and cancer.

Percent of Death From Specified Causes by Sex and Age, 1972
Metropolitan Life Insurance Company—Standard Ordinary
Policyholders

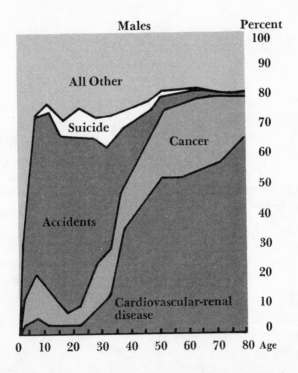

Metropolitan Life Insurance Company *Statistical Bulletin,*
March 1973

The preceding graph serves to clearly point out this fact, and one can see why health hazard appraisal can assist in the development of preventive plans for different age groups. In the 1972 Metropolitan Life Insurance Company data, more than 50 percent of the male deaths between ages five through twenty-four were due to accidents and suicide. Among those over thirty-five, however, heart disease and cancer were the conditions that required the greatest preventive attention. Within each of these major groupings are a whole series of health hazards that change in importance as we move through life. If properly identified, measures can be taken to cope with them just as has been done in *A Parents' Guide to Child Safety.*

In his book, Dr. Fontana has brought to parents and the public a long-needed document that identifies the hazards and points out ways to avoid them or to handle them if they occur. Most people consider it instinctive for parents to want to ensure an environment for growing children that is free from undue risk or injury. On the surface, it would also seem that the protection of the child from physical harm would require the most simple of safety precautions. Yet, as Dr. Fontana has so forcefully pointed out, it is in this area of accident prevention that we have failed so miserably. Why should this be? And what can we do to improve our chances for success in the future? As my wife, Beth, and I discussed the subject we could not help but identify closely with almost every accident described. Since we have a large family ourselves, many of the hazardous situations presented actually occurred within our own family group. We have had a child struck by a car, one bitten by a vicious dog, a dislocated elbow from a fall, and innumerable others that we may have been ignorant of or that perhaps are yet to come. One might ask how this could happen in a family whose parents should know how to avoid such calamities.

Going back over the years and analyzing several of the more serious mishaps, we became aware that we really had not perceived the potential dangers that exist when a combination of factors can turn a safe situation into a disaster. In one case, for example, our now twenty-seven-year-old son, when age two, drank from a soft-drink bottle containing kerosene. Emergency care averted any complications, but the close call was terrifying. You may wonder why we ever permitted such an unsafe situation to occur in the first place. Quite simply, safety-proofing of our own home included ruling the combination of soda bottles and kerosene as a "no-no." Never did we entertain the possibility, however, that such might not be the case at our neighbors', where we were visiting. What we learned was a lesson for new parents—be more cautious when your children are in new environments. Even a visit to Grandma's house may present its problems. It is a rare grandparent indeed who can remain completely attuned to the mischievousness and adventuresome ways of children. I remember, in particular, the occasion when a handsome glass towel rod in Grandma's bathroom became a swinging bar for our rambunctious three-year-old son. Even with his mother in direct observation, the accident occurred so fast that the broken rod and several lacerated arteries in the arm became history in the time it took to blink an eye. Once again, quick first aid and a good surgeon saved the day and, in this case, a life. The lesson learned was similar to that in the first case—make a safety survey when in new surroundings. Fortunately, safety laws have also been enacted as a result of such accidents. In many states, hazardous glass rods, doors, and windows must now meet safety design criteria before being marketed.

I might add that this young lad did survive growing up and even played professional football for several years prior to entering law school. He continued, however, to be one of the more accident-prone of our eleven children. On one occasion, after learning about solid carbon dioxide and dry ice in his school science class, he tried some experimentation on his own. After deftly inserting pieces of dry ice into a pop bottle, it wasn't long until the pressure built up in the bottle was sufficient to cause shattering. The resultant lacerations of his hands finally healed without causing disability after a considerable amount of secondary infection was cleared up. The moral of this story is that one must practice eternal vigilance, not only by sight but also in the mind's eye. If a child can think of it, you'd better believe that sooner or later he may try it!

The many other close calls, mishaps and unsafe acts that Beth and I are aware of could fill a book. Those that have happened but that we didn't know about could, I feel certain, fill a shelf! In either case, however, I am sure that a close analysis of the accident or unsafe behavior would have clearly pointed out the action necessary to have prevented a disaster or unsafe situation from occurring. I am equally sure, however, that you would agree with me that there is no real pat or absolute solution to most safety problems. Solutions are, at best, a result of compromises. A number of these will become self-evident as you read the ensuing chapters.

It is also well to remember that life is inherently risky, and to a great extent, this is what gives it its zest. Our real aim is to give our children sufficient guidance so that they can wind their way through life's hazards with an optimum amount of freedom from injury or risk. A child who is given too many no's and don'ts may well become a timid and ineffective person or perhaps one who revolts completely and throws all caution to the wind. All of us in life have a job to do. The job at hand for the child is to reach maturity. Overprotective accident prevention may displace knowledge required for growing up. Do not allow your children to become masters of what not to do. Life is not oriented toward such goals. The use of the words *no* and *don't* should be assigned high values. Their use should be rationed for those occasions where serious danger or risk of injury might otherwise prevail.

For a guideline on the positive side of accident prevention, consider the following: Design a child's early experiences to be success oriented; reduce his exposure to error and unsafe conditions. Always emphasize that a job well done is inherently safe. Finally, if there is one thing that we should not only impart to the young but heed ourselves, it is this: Learn from the mistakes of others; we won't live long enough to make them all ourselves. With a ten-year-old still in the nest, we will have, you can be assured, childhood safety as an intimate part of our lives for a number of years to come.

Contents

Preface

In our lifetime, we have been witness to some of the greatest medical achievements in mankind's history. The most noteworthy examples are the progressive decrease in childhood deaths due to infections, and the prolongation of life. These advances are largely due to the discovery of new immunization procedures against contagious diseases, emphasis on preventive care for children, and the advent of more effective antibiotics and other life-saving drugs. However, in spite of these wonderful medical breakthroughs, accidents remain the most common cause of death in children.

The National Research Council has stated that the federal government, most doctors, and the general public are all guilty of apathy and neglect for not taking any positive steps to arrest this terrifying prevalence of accidental injury and death in our society. The council further noted that "this neglected epidemic of modern society is the nation's most important environmental problem. It is the leading cause of death in the first half of life's span."

It has been estimated that 14,000 children under the age of fifteen die each year in this country from accidents.

The mortality rate is probably higher since many deaths due to accidental injury are not reported. Approximately 17 million children are injured at some time or another during their early childhood. Each year a total of 50,000 children are crippled and almost 2 million are temporarily incapacitated by accidental injury. One child out of every three is injured severely enough each year in the United States to require medical attention; as a result, the child's activities are restricted for days or even months. Death due to injury is highest in the group of children under five years. During any one year, the statisticians tell us, 5,500 accidental deaths in children under five years of age occur in the home. Most accidental deaths in the five-to-fourteen age group are caused by motor vehicles; in almost half these accidents the child victim is a pedestrian. Another 13 percent of fatal accidents are caused when children's bikes collide with automobiles; and more than 500 children lose their lives every year as a result of shootings. Next in order of occurrence come drownings, fire and burns, falls, railroad mishaps, and poisonings.

The growing mass of statistics that is being accumulated on accidental deaths in children is shocking. The medical profession has been slow in recognizing accident prevention as one of the major health problems affecting the American people. The plain fact is that accidents, whether inside or outside the home, are the number-one threat to the life and safety of any child. Parents must be well informed and alert to possible danger so that they may constitute the first line of defense against accidental injury to their children.

The home environment poses the greatest hazard to the child. It is somewhat difficult to understand or accept the paradox that what should be the most secure environment for a child can also be the most life-threatening. In our modern and affluent society, this important public health problem is still unsolved. It is a sad commentary that death due to accidents in children is 175 percent higher than the most common medical cause of deaths, namely, cancer. This fact alone should generate the type of concern for human life that befits a society that pretends to care so much for its children.

There really is no need for a child to die from suffocation, accidental trauma, or poisoning. Efforts are being made and have been made in the past to enlighten the public. The Committee on Accident Prevention of the American Academy of Pediatrics has assisted the medical profession in the areas of accident prevention, particularly with reference to lead intoxication and drug poisoning.

Burns involving clothing fires constitute a significant portion of the accident problem. In the United States, an estimated 3,000 deaths and 150,000 injuries occur annually from burning clothing. Injuries resulting from exposure to ignited clothing are most prevalent in children. As a result of these burn deaths and injuries to children, the Flammable Fabrics Act was enacted and became effective on July 1, 1954. The purpose of the act is to reduce the danger of injury and loss of life by providing, on a national basis, regulations designed to discourage the use of dangerously flammable clothing textiles.

Poison control centers have been established in every part of the United States providing physicians and parents with instant identification of the poisonous ingredients in common household products and directions for emergency treatment. They are comprehensively listed by states in Appendix A.

Pediatricians have distributed thousands of *Child Safety Suggestion Guides* prepared by the Committee on Accident Prevention. The use of these *Guides* has helped reduce the incidence of childhood accidents, and countless numbers of children have had their lives spared. But the tragic apathy of most parents remains.

Although some progress has been made, in view of the statistics that become available year after year we are far from accomplishing what ought to be done. The reasons for this slow progress lie in a number of areas: lack of professional interest; society's ignorance of the problem; and parental apathy. But the key factor, and the one we have not discussed, is parents' inability to recognize and practice loving discipline.

Accidents have causes. The most puzzling part about the accident does not appear to be *how* the child incurred the accident, but *why* the child actually had it. That is, did the accident occur because of parental neglect, abuse, lack of supervision, or simply because of carelessness? It must be remembered that accidents do not just "happen" —they are caused and they can be prevented.

In his traditional role in matters of child health and welfare, the pediatrician has an understandable concern about children's deaths and the irreparable physical damage that is produced by accidents. However, there is also an unequivocal parental responsibility in the field of childhood accidents that has prompted the writing of this book for all concerned parents of young children. We are dealing with a problem that cannot be handled by doctors alone since it directly involves the heart of our society and demands parental concern and involvement.

Acknowledgments

Much of the material in this book has been gathered through the skilled research efforts of Miss Lee Fontana; without her work this book would not be as complete as it is. My deep appreciation to Mrs. Loretta Carr for her secretarial assistance. Last but not least, the publication of this book would not have been possible without the help of my dedicated personal secretary, Miss Anne Dougherty.

1

The Whys and Wherefores of Childhood Accidents

Parents, especially mothers, show an outpouring of affection and concern for the child who is threatened with an illness. The pediatrician is consulted at any hour of the day. Parents read books on baby care and take the child to the pediatrician for all his immunizations and feeding instructions. However, some of these parents fail to show a similar interest in protecting their children from accidents by taking the simple precautions necessary to prevent them. Many of the common childhood diseases have been conquered by the use of antibiotics and preventive immunizations. On the other hand, the decrease in accidental death rates in children has been alarmingly slow; accidental deaths have decreased only half as rapidly as deaths from infectious diseases. Unfortunately, there are no vaccines that can protect children against accidents—only careful supervision.

Accidents involve human behavior, both individual and collective. Human behavior is strongly influenced by training and disciplinary measures experienced in early childhood. The resultant individual human behavior causes or prevents accidents.

The interplay of attitudes between parent and child—

physical, mental, and emotional—is also at the root of many accidents. Accidents are often caused by a sequence of events rather than by a single factor. The child who is guided by a spirit of adventure and daring poses a high risk, especially if an air of independence and experimentation is also present. The child who is hungry, irritated, frustrated, or angry is also more likely to get into trouble if the circumstances permit. It is not always easy to recognize when children are under stress and therefore may be more vulnerable to accidental injury.

The family that is unstable also contributes to the potential for accidents within the home. Marital discord, financial distress, older children's drug addiction, and other stressful situations within the family lead to parental preoccupation, faulty supervision, and neglect. Investigators have noted that one of the significant factors contributing to childhood accidents is the emotional and physical condition of the mother at the time of the mishap. One study indicated that the mothers of more than half of the youngsters involved in accidents were ill, pregnant, or menstruating at the time. An equally large percentage of mothers were under emotional tension caused by poor marital and financial conditions.

In the past, a child's behavior was considered to be determined largely by genes and heredity. Parents' difficulties and guilts were therefore greatly relieved as they considered the behavior of their child. However, today it is fairly well accepted that a child's behavior is determined as well by his environment.

A child's development begins immediately after birth. As he grows, his parents protect him from dangerous substances and medicines. He is warned against dangerous weapons, matches, hot stoves, boiling pots. He hears a multitude of don'ts. However, parents may fail to employ one very significant preventive measure: discipline. Discipline is essential to every child's security and protection. The child must learn that his own interest is best served by following parental directions. The lack of a tender, loving type of discipline has been recognized as a major factor in many cases of childhood injury. The child must be taught the limits of his own freedom. Discipline should be consistent, justified, understandable, but not excessive. It must sometimes be gentle, sometimes firm, but always administered with assurance. Parents should be accepting and loving despite the child's disobedience. Excessive discipline that a child cannot understand can lead to accidents.

Disciplinary measures indicate to the child parental disapproval of an action. This type of discipline must be understandable to the child so that his own interests are best served by following the course directed by his parents. In this way, the child will appreciate that his parents will not permit him to hurt himself in any way and he will thereby learn self-discipline, common sense, and sound judgment.

Protect, but don't overprotect your child. Bumps, bruises, and falls are the necessary signposts on the path to growing up and learning. The child who is continuously prevented from any sort of ordinary play because of some emotional instability on the part of the parents is apt to get into difficulties. Children can be taught to respond to the command "no" if it is not overused to the point of losing its effectiveness. The inflection, intonation, timing, and spirit of the command are all important if the message is to register in the child's mind.

Many accidents happen because parents are unaware

of their child's physical capabilities at a specific age of development. One young mother left her child alone in the backyard for a few minutes to answer a telephone call. Since the yard was surrounded by a high fence, the mother was confident that her son would be safe until her return. Minutes later she returned outside, but her child was nowhere in sight. She searched and called his name. Finally it occurred to her to look into the 4-foot-deep, above-ground pool with a stepladder against its side, standing in the corner of the yard. She knew the child could not climb the ladder; he was fourteen months old. When in desperation she decided to look in, she saw her son—floating in the water. A lack of understanding of his physical capabilities led to this child's drowning. His mother assumed that since the child could not walk, he could not climb a stepladder. But in young children, spurts of development may occur overnight; they may be crawling one day, walking the next. Perhaps if his mother had kept one step ahead of her curious son—who was so attracted to the potential hazard—a life might have been saved. Understand your child's ever-changing needs and his physical and mental development. Keep one step ahead of your youngster so that you can expect the unexpected.

Understanding his own child and knowing what children are like in a general way will help strengthen the parent's control of the situation and increase his ability to recognize the child's need for discipline. Children grow physically and emotionally, some faster than others and some more than others. The sexes are different in their reactions, with boys usually more likely to get into accidents than girls. This is perhaps due to the fact that boys tend to be more active, aggressive, and daring and are more likely to take risks, sometimes in an effort to show off. Of course there are some girls who go through a tomboyish phase and will be as prone to accidents as boys.

During infancy the mobility of the child continues to increase so that between the ages of one and two years he is more prone to encounter accidental injury, and for this reason this phase of his life is often referred to as the "age of accidents." During this very active period of his life, he can climb out a window or out of his crib, chew electrical cords, stick pins in live outlets, open doors and fall downstairs, reach for drugs and poisons, choke on foods, start fires, drown easily in his bath or swimming pool,

pull boiling water from the stove down on himself, or crawl or run into the path of a car.

As the child grows, his world expands, his curiosity increases, and the possibility of accidents also increases. The child spends more hours outdoors investigating the universe and asking the whys and wherefores of his every-day encounters. His senses of touch and taste are also developing—perhaps more than his sense of danger—so that with the inquisitive urge present in the preschooler he sets out to taste and touch whatever is in easy reach. By touching, smelling, and tasting the objects around him, a child learns and grows. The world becomes a play-ground of new shapes and tastes. The area in which he plays can be a safe one in which to grow—but only if the parents make it so.

When a child reaches school age, his parents may dis-cover that the child they thought "clumsy" or "accident-prone" is unable to hear or see too well. They may have directed him to avoid an accident, only to be ignored. They may have thought him disobedient. During a complete preschool physical examination a child's hearing defect or poor eyesight may be diagnosed for the first time. The simple removal of wax from a child's ear may make him aware of what you are saying—and lo and behold he becomes an obedient child. Defective vision can cause your child to blink, rub his eyes, squint, frown, or lacrimate—these signs of poor eyesight could cause an accidental injury. A parent must recognize the clues to either an eyesight or hearing problem and check with the family physician—who may refer him to an ophthalmologist (an eye specialist) or an otologist (an expert in the detection of hearing loss).

Certain children have been described as "accident repeaters" because for some reason they are frequently involved in mishaps, and parents often ask whether some children are really more accident-prone than others. Studies have been made to find out why some children are "always getting into accidents" and in what ways they differ from other children. An interesting five-year study of these children showed that they were indeed accident-prone; however, their mishaps were not purposeful and not the result of any self-destructive psychological behavior. The researchers found that these children had frequent accidents because of their preoccupation with other things and not because of any psychological disturbance.

How then can a parent best help a child who is constantly getting into accidents? He should first ease up on the youngster. The parent should reassure the child, forget his shortcomings for the moment, and instill in him confidence and self-assurance. Let him know that you are pleased with him just as he is. With parental approval, a child's talents and inclinations will fruitfully develop, and accidents that can occur because of distractability, anger, or dissatisfaction with oneself will be prevented. In this way, the accident-prone child is likely to become nonaccident-prone.

Children develop and learn what is expected of them by imitating their elders. Parents become examples for the child's future actions: The growing child tries hard to emulate and please his parents. He identifies with the persons who take care of him and teach him. The three-to-five-year-old is receptive to learning experiences and is capable of comprehending more than his parents usually believe he can. He can easily be taught to swim, to cross the street carefully, to climb trees without accident, and many other meaningful accident-preventive actions.

A young child must be taught to think for himself if he is to be able to cope with the unexpected. Parents must also prepare a child to handle emergencies without being frightened. A good time to prepare a young child for the unexpected is when he is in a familiar situation. Simple instructions are the best, such as what to do if he becomes lost on his way home and how to dial for help on a telephone.

As the child grows and goes to school, he is away from the home and the watchful eye of his mother. He is forced to develop independent thoughts and ideas and engage in independent actions. He thus becomes far more responsible for his own safety. The philosopher Carl Becker has stated: "Since I was free to do as I please, I was responsible for what it was that I was pleased to do." This does not mean that the child always knows what he should do or that he is able to do what he should do. Responsible judgment is not a characteristic that is developed under constant supervision and modification. Responsibility must be learned first by parents who then pass the trait on to their children. A child's responsibility is then supported by school and childhood experiences. Personal responsibility can only be passed on to future generations by nurture and active example. Judgment is something that is developed; we are not born with it.

Adult leadership in accident prevention plays an important role during the early school years. It has been aptly stated that children are only as safe as their supervision causes them to be. Have you ever made a quick dash to the store while your small children were playing or watching TV? Have you ever visited your next-door neighbor while your children were taking a nap? How often have you taken one of your children to school, or to a doctor's or dentist's appointment, leaving your other children alone for a few minutes? Unfortunately, all parents take chances at one time or another and leave a child home alone. Thousands of children are killed or maimed for life every year because of lack of supervision. Take your young children with you on all your errands, or leave them with a competent baby-sitter or older family member. Small children need constant supervision and are practically helpless in an emergency without adult aid.

The total practical approach to accident prevention, therefore, involves protecting the child during his early development, teaching him to avoid dangers, and making his environment safer. Accidents can and must be prevented. The most promising solution to the problem of accidental injury and death is to make it possible for all parents to participate actively in a society more earnestly dedicated to accident prevention. This challenge can be infinitely rewarding. Are you willing to accept this challenge?

2

Childhood Poisonings

Accidental poisoning fatalities in childhood constitute an increasing problem. The National Safety Council stated in a recent report that an estimated 4,600 Americans died from poisoning in 1970. In 1973, 500,000 children will swallow poisonous materials found in their homes and about 400 will die as a result. The majority of these accidental deaths are due to poisoning from drugs, household cleansing agents, a variety of foodstuffs, and gases. These poisonings, when combined with accidents, account for the largest number of deaths in the pediatric age group, and together account for more fatalities than the next seven leading causes of death combined. In point of fact, in the United States the number of deaths resulting from poisoning in children under five years of age is four times higher than in Great Britain.

Practically all of the childhood poisoning deaths are caused by the ingestion of poisons contained in household agents of all kinds, of which some 250,000 are commonly used. These agents are all potentially dangerous poisons and an estimated 40,000 new trade names enter the marketplace every year. The frequency of accidents can only increase with the discovery of new drugs and the even

greater diffusion of numerous chemicals and pharmaceutical preparations used in the treatment of disease. These substances include frequently used drugs such as tranquilizers, sedatives, antibiotics, and pain killers.

Children under five are curious and fearless; they are too young to read labels or to understand warnings and are quick to accidentally ingest household items. The great majority of children in this age bracket are intrigued and attracted by products that are left within their reach. Nearly 50 percent of all poisonings occur in this age group. Children under five years of age are "crawlers" and "climbers" and "searchers." They cannot make the slightest distinction between what is dangerous and what is not. They find products stored under the kitchen sink, in medicine cabinets, on shelves, windowsills, dressers, tables, and even in handbags. Children at this age are a particularly high risk and extremely vulnerable to accidental poisoning. In 1970, over 12,000 ingested cleaning fluid, polishing agents, detergents, disinfectants, bleaches, and insecticides—products that were kept in cabinets or under sinks. The danger is compounded under certain circumstances such as moving, repairing, housepainting, spring-cleaning, or during special preparations for a sick person or house guest. Clearly, then, this is an extremely dangerous period when parents should be especially alert.

A typical story of accidental poisoning involves a three-year-old child who went to bed as usual along with his brothers and sisters. Later that night, after the others were asleep, he got up, climbed onto the kitchen clothes dryer, and reached into the linen closet where the family aspirin was kept. His mother, for safety reasons, had hidden it there, never suspecting that one day the children could reach the shelf by climbing. The child found the aspirin and swallowed an unknown number of tablets—but he was lucky. His mother, a light sleeper, heard noises, found him in time, and rushed him to the hospital. Other children have not been as fortunate as this child. There was the two-year-old who swallowed some beads from a broken poison-berry necklace that belonged to her older sister, and the two-year-old who inhaled talcum powder while playing with the container and died of pneumonia.

Another child, four years old, watched her mother polishing a table; the telephone rang and her mother left the room to answer it. On her return, a few minutes later, she found that the child had drunk some of the furniture polish and poisoned herself. The sad stories continue: A commercial artist was painting a sign for a local merchant at home. He left the room to answer the phone, and by the time he returned his young son had taken a fatal drink from a jar of kerosine used to clean brushes that was on the father's worktable. Another mother was cleaning a blouse when she heard a ring at the door, which she went to open, and while she was gone her two-year-old child drank the contents of the bottle of cleaning fluid.

These tragic stories illustrate what can happen to a child who moves fast when a parent's back is turned. Over 75 percent of accidents happen when a parent or baby-sitter is called away and the child is left alone with a potential poison, even for a few seconds.

Accidental poisonings are entirely the result of inadequate and improper supervision in an unsafe environment. No chemical agents are entirely safe and all should be considered potentially harmful. The severity of the poisoning is dependent upon the nature of the poison and the amount allowed to come in contact with the body.

Potentially toxic substances are killers of children and pose one of the most serious problems in everyday living. During President Lyndon B. Johnson's tenure of office, the concern of the federal government was expressed by the President's statement that "an untold number of innocent children, who are too young and inexperienced to comprehend their peril, are needlessly and thoughtlessly exposed to grave injury, or even death, as a result of the careless or negligent handling and storage and disposal by adults of potentially poisonous medicine and household products."

Parents are the first line of defense against accidental

poisoning. Be aware of the dangers in your home and take steps to make it poison-proof. Preventive measures taken now can prevent a future tragedy in your home.

The Poisons

ASPIRIN

Aspirin, known also as acetylsalicylic acid, is an important medication purchased without a doctor's prescription. It is used daily for a variety of complaints and is safe when taken as directed. More aspirin is ingested every year than any other drug. However, few parents recognize its potential danger. When ingested in excessive amounts, aspirin is certainly a dangerous drug and a potential cause of death in children. Unfortunately, in order to get them to take it, all too often parents will tell their children that aspirin is candy. These parents are asking for trouble. The child may at a later date seek out the "candy" and consume large quantities of it. Of the 5,767 incidents of aspirin poisoning reported by the Public Health Service Poison Control Branch in 1970, eight out of ten cases involved a candy-flavored aspirin.

A not unfamiliar story is that of a mother who was skeptical when her two-year-old child appeared in the living room and announced proudly, "I ate up all the candy." The orange-flavored children's aspirin was kept out of Susan's reach, so her mother went along with the

story. "Really?" she said. "Where did you find it?" She followed her daughter to the kitchen. The child pointed to the high cabinet shelf where the aspirin was kept. "And how did you reach it?" the mother asked, knowing that even the counter below the cabinet was out of the child's reach. "I'll show you," Susan said. Her mother watched, and Susan pulled the chair across the room, mounted it, climbed from there to the countertop, and scaled the cabinet shelf by shelf. "See?" she cried proudly, presenting the aspirin bottle, completely empty, and minus its so-called safety cap. The child was immediately rushed to the emergency room of a hospital where her stomach was pumped. A large quantity of aspirin was removed, and the child survived. This is a typical example wherein a mother who felt she had done everything to protect her child had not really taken the mental and physical prowess of the child into consideration.

Manufacturers of aspirin began to package orange-flavored baby aspirin several years ago. In 1968, they put safety closures on baby-aspirin bottles and decreased the number of tablets from fifty to thirty-six. The result was that there were fewer children swallowing big doses of aspirin than before. In 1970, the Poison Prevention Act required that all aspirin and products containing aspirin be sold to the consumer in a container with a safety closure. The manufacturers' voluntary packaging of children's aspirin in bottles of not more than thirty-six tablets has certainly decreased serious episodes of accidentally ingested aspirin poisoning since such an overdose of aspirin could not be fatal. However, it is important to keep in mind that children can *get to* and ingest any type of aspirin tablet whether it be in containers of thirty-five or a hundred, and whether it be baby aspirin or adult size.

Those interested in accident prevention have suggested that aspirin be marketed with each tablet wrapped separately in cellophane strips as are some other medications. But to date this practice is not widespread, and, of course, no amount of legislation concerning safety containers or specific types of packaging will stop the accidental poisoning of children unless the parents do everything that must be done. And it is worth emphasizing over and over again that eternal vigilance is the only means of protecting small children and assuring their safety from accidental poisoning.

It is important for parents not to use the word "candy" when giving medication, especially aspirin. Keep aspirin —which is not an "innocent" drug—in a locked medicine cabinet out of the reach of children. Last but not least, know the potential of your child and what he is capable of doing under certain circumstances.

LEAD

Since ancient times lead has been known to cause poisoning in man. However, only in recent years have we discovered that lead can have a toxic effect on children. A child's ingestion of flakes of lead paint is sad testimony to our inability to completely control and prevent this type of poisoning. In the United States alone, about 400,000 children are victims of lead poisoning each year. An estimated 200 of these children die and another 800 suffer physical damage necessitating permanent care. Every year, if present statistics continue, approximately 3,200 children will suffer moderate to severe brain damage secondary to the excessive ingestion of lead.

Children between the ages of one and six years are the main victims. Many of these children have what is called "pica"—an unnatural craving for inedible nonfood substances. These children usually pick up and eat chips of lead-containing paint that they find on floors or on peeling walls. Most cribs and toys today are no longer a source of lead poisoning. The vast majority of manufacturers now use paint free of lead or with a lead content of less than 1 percent for indoor painting. Paint having a high lead content is usually found on walls in old tenements in which new coats of paint have been applied over old ones without prior scraping.

Certain physical signs develop if a child has ingested a significant amount of lead. Anemia may be present. The child may complain of muscular weakness, dizziness, difficulty in seeing. He may even have convulsive seizures. The higher the blood level of lead, the more severe are the symptoms, and if a child is allowed to continue without treatment, complicating symptoms, such as lethargy, twitchings, and coma, involving the central nervous system appear.

One unfortunate victim of lead poisoning was a child of six. Formerly bright and congenial, he had spoken in sentences at the age of two, and soon afterward tried to read. But at the age of six his teacher found him to be irritable, hyperactive, difficult, uncooperative, and moody. His parents turned to the pediatrician, who subsequently referred the child to a psychiatrist. The psychiatrist diagnosed the child's condition as minimal brain damage and prescribed treatment with a stimulant-type drug that had a calming effect on him. Although the drug seemed to curb the boy's difficult behavior, his learning difficulties were still evident. Another consultant psychiatrist indicated that there could be a possible connection between his learning disability and the abnormally high level of lead that was found in his blood on testing. This proved to be the case.

Children are the high-risk members of our society for lead poisoning. Proper prevention of this type of poisoning is dependent on an informed and concerned parent. The parent must see that a test for lead poisoning is done on any child who has been exposed to paint or other materials containing lead and who suffers convulsive seizures or shows signs of nervousness or irritability. Parents must be aware of the dangers of lead poisoning to avoid the complications that can result if the diagnosis is not made early.

KEROSENE AND
PETROLEUM DISTILLATES

About a quarter of the fatal poisonings of children are due to kerosene and other petroleum distillates; 80 percent of the victims are children under five years of age. It has been estimated that nearly 28,000 nonfatal poisonings due to petroleum distillates occur annually in children under five years of age in the United States.

One victim was a two-year-old boy whose mother was polishing furniture. When she momentarily put the bottle of polish down, the child picked it up and ingested about two ounces of the contents. The boy vomited spontaneously and afterward was taken to the hospital where his stomach was pumped out. During his stay in the hospital, the boy developed pneumonia. In spite of the complications, the story has a happy ending. The child recovered and was discharged after several weeks' treatment.

The accidental ingestion of kerosene and other petroleum distillates is aided and abetted by the fact that often these substances are removed from their original containers to be put into drinking glasses, bottles, and jars, and left where children can reach them and swallow the contents very easily.

Our surroundings, both indoors and outdoors, are filled with petroleum-distillate products. We use them in cleaning, painting, exterminating insects and pests, and in a wide variety of other ways to make life easier. Whether they make life safer is another question, since these substances have a potential for great harm to children.

Substances that are used every day and are frequently available in the home are the ones that are most likely to cause accidental poisoning when ingested by infants and children. These substances include heating fuels, solvents, cleaning fluids, insecticides, paint thinners, cigarette lighter fluid, gasoline, benzine, and kerosene. The chief symptoms of petroleum poisoning are burning of the mouth, throat, and esophagus, and nausea, vomiting, coughing, diarrhea, drowsiness, depression, dizziness, difficulty in breathing, convulsions, and coma.

In poisoning due to petroleum-distillate products do not attempt to clean out the stomach or induce vomiting under any circumstance. As a result of such treatment, the child could develop an aspiration pneumonia, as well as suffer damage to the mouth, throat, and esophagus. *It is strongly recommended that the child suffering from petroleum-distillate poisoning be given emergency measures as indicated on pages 34–35.*

GASOLINE ADDICTION

Another real hazard that must be recognized by parents is the potential in children for developing an addiction to gasoline. Easy access to gasoline and a certain personality syndrome in the child may result in this condition. Gasoline addicts are usually boys in a home environment that is unsettled owing to marital discord or violence. Divorce, threatened or actual, is often a feature in such a family unit. These children sometimes find a way to relieve their tensions by the inhalation of gasoline, which produces a state of drunken euphoria. Children who succumb to this addiction become psychologically dependent on the gasoline and induce intoxication to relieve their anxiety.

In one reported case, an eleven-year-old boy was hospitalized for what was initially believed to be an acute schizophrenic episode. Four days before his hospitalization, his father had discovered him with his mouth over the opening of a gasoline can. Another boy of fourteen who admitted he was addicted to gasoline revealed that he had started sniffing gasoline at the age of three years and did it whenever he became anxious. From the age of six years on, the patient had recurrent prolonged bouts of gasoline inhalation that he continued until he passed out.

These cases give evidence that gasoline addiction can be a real problem for some parents and for those children who, to attract attention or for reasons of loneliness or self-centeredness, will fall into a gasoline-addiction problem.

GLUE SNIFFING

Glue sniffing among children and adolescents has become a serious problem throughout the nation. This practice is widespread among some teen-agers and is considered a serious problem by physicians, school officials, and law-enforcement agencies. It may begin by the inhalation of the vapor from a variety of plastic cements or glues, which produces dizziness associated with some mild euphoria, dream states, and hallucinations. The child puts the glue into a plastic or waxed paper bag and holds it to his nose. A series of deep breaths rapidly brings on a pleasant euphoria. If continued over long periods of time, this type of inhalation causes serious damage to the blood system, kidneys, and liver. The overall effect of inhaling the glue vapor is an immediate acute brain syndrome resembling alcohol intoxication with the addition of more serious side effects leading to deterioration of judgment, accidental injury, and, at times, death.

Parents must understand that glue sniffing is not a game. It is not usually an isolated event and should not be overlooked. Although true addiction in the sense of addiction to heroin is not found, the child's psychological attitude may cause him to continue his practice of glue sniffing and, under certain circumstances, combine with it alcohol ingestion or the use of other addicting drugs such as barbiturates and heroin.

Children usually sniff glue in such secluded places as the family basement, apartment house roofs, alleys, or in the restrooms of elementary and high schools. Children are often introduced to the drug by a "dare" to try it, or the habit may begin through curiosity after they have read about the practice. They buy the glue with money given them by their parents or they may occasionally steal to obtain it.

One ten-year-old boy reported that he and his playmates developed the habit of inhaling the glue they used in assembling model toys. This child gave a fine description of the results of sniffing. He stated that he became "dizzy, dopey, and talked funny." After that he passed out for half a minute to a minute and a half.

What can be done to prevent glue sniffing? Perhaps through legislation public health agencies may enlist the aid of industry in using safer solvents in the manufacture of glue and cements. A more potent weapon perhaps is improving the social conditions that lead to addiction as well as alerting physicians, children, parents, and the community at large to the potential dangers of glue sniffing.

Parents must remember that glue sniffing, like alcoholism, gasoline inhalation, or drug addiction, is symptomatic of an underlying emotional disturbance or personality disorder in the child. If the child engages in this undesirable practice, the parents must seek professional help in order to take whatever steps are necessary to alleviate the underlying emotional tension that can drive a child to this type of addiction, which can of course lead to serious accidental injury or death.

DETERGENTS AND CLEANING AGENTS

A great variety of detergents and cleaning materials is found in every home in America. The toxicity and dangers associated with these common household products are related to their irritant and caustic—burning—properties. Electric dishwasher detergent granules may be severely caustic. Soluble water softeners are also potentially caustic. Some commercial detergents have been found to have a high alkaline content, which, if ingested, produces severe corrosive injury to the stomach and esophagus. (Fortunately, small amounts of detergents that accidentally come into contact with the body rarely cause any illness or discomfort.) Other corrosive materials include strong alkalis commonly used in drainpipe cleaners, paint removers, and other strong cleansing agents.

Fifteen percent of all inquiries to poison control centers throughout the country involve questions concerning the accidental ingestion of household detergents by children under five years of age. Presently steps are being taken by government and industry to have detergents of high alkalinity sold only in safety packages. Products threatening caustic effects are usually identified with a CAUTION or WARNING label. Parents should make an effort to select the least hazardous brand of detergent, especially if there are small children in the home.

LYE

The ingestion of lye by children under five years of age is an extremely serious problem. Liquid drain cleaners contain sodium hydroxide and potassium hydroxide, highly toxic substances that, when accidentally ingested, cause burns and subsequent scarring of the esophagus. As a result, periodic surgical intervention becomes necessary to dilate the scars in the esophagus.

CLEANING FLUID
(CARBON TETRACHLORIDE)

Cleaning fluid (the chemical name for which is carbon tetrachloride) is a household product that is effective in removing oil stains and grease. Despite its widespread use, few parents realize that this substance is one of the most toxic substances used in the household. Swallowing only a teaspoonful of carbon tetrachloride has caused death. It can also be absorbed directly through the skin or inhaled.

One mother recently used half a cup of carbon tetrachloride to clean the upholstery of two chairs. That afternoon her five-year-old son came home from school with a slight cold and sat on one of the chairs to watch television. Later the child became violently ill and was taken to the hospital. The cause of his illness was the continuous inhaling of the poisonous vapors of the carbon tetrachloride remaining on the chair.

The toxicity of this chemical has been recognized by manufacturers so that all carbon tetrachloride containers are labeled POISON, MAY BE FATAL IF INHALED OR SWALLOWED. To avoid a catastrophe, use other less toxic cleaning fluids that are not dangerous to you or your children, and store them under lock and key.

MOTHBALLS

Innocent-looking mothballs may look like candy to some children. Mothballs are used in some homes to discourage moths in clothing and overstuffed furniture. They are also often found on floors and in stored carpeting for protection against humidity. These practices encourage mothball ingestion by children.

Another real hazard is passing "hand-me-downs" from one sibling to another after they have been stored for a long period of time with naphthalene and mothballs. A mother recently brought an eleven-day-old infant to the hospital because she noted that the child appeared jaundiced for three days, and the jaundice, or yellow coloring of the skin, had been getting progressively worse. She also noticed that the infant's urine was dark, like tea. There was no vomiting, fever, or other sign of illness, and after a thorough examination the doctors could not discover the reason for the jaundice. However, when they questioned the mother further, she revealed that she had dressed the child in clothes that had been stored in 100 percent pure naphthalene for over a year.

If hand-me-downs are used, the clothing must first be laundered and thoroughly aired before being passed on to another sibling. Better still, don't take a chance—keep mothballs out of the home completely.

BABY POWDER

Baby powder, used by mothers as a dusting agent for the newborn and younger child, can become a source of tragedy in the home. Talcum powder can cause a very serious type of pneumonia. It is easily accessible, frequently used, and often within easy reach of the child. Some mothers will even allow a child to hold and play with a talcum powder container as a means of pacifying

him. Children should not be allowed to play with powder of any type. Receptacles containing baby powder should never be left in the crib or on a table near the crib.

PESTICIDES

Hundreds of children die every year from swallowing or coming into contact with poisons designed to kill insects, weeds, or rodents. Because some children become only mildly ill, parents may fail to recognize the symptoms of pesticide poisoning. Each year, 40,000 to 50,000 cases of such nonfatal poisonings are reported in the

United States, some of them of course mild, others very severe. These figures are applicable only to poisons taken by mouth. Poisons inhaled or absorbed through the skin are not usually reported and the incidence of such poisoning is unknown. The California Department of Public Health has in its files the case of a child who died less than ten minutes after merely dipping her finger in a container of concentrated tetraethylpyrophosphate (TEPP).

Evidence over the years points to the fact that most pesticide accidents are the result of gross carelessness on the part of parents who may disregard and not fully appreciate the fact that they are bringing into the home a potentially lethal chemical that must be properly labeled and stored under lock and key.

> Accidental deaths of children due to pesticides can be prevented by following certain precautionary measures:
> 1. Lock up all pesticides when not in use.
> 2. Put empty aerosol spray-type dispensers in rubbish immediately.
> 3. Never put poisons in pop bottles or any other familiar type of container that will attract a small child.

CARBON MONOXIDE

Carbon monoxide has been called the "silent killer" because it is a colorless, odorless, and tasteless gas. It is estimated that each year at least 10,000 persons suffer chronic ill effects from exposure to sublethal but debilitating levels of carbon monoxide. Children are frequently the victims of carbon monoxide poisoning.

The most frequently encountered cause of carbon monoxide poisoning is the innocent-looking culprit, the unvented gas heater. Without a constant supply of fresh air, a gas heater will burn less efficiently. If there is no vent to carry off the carbon monoxide produced, it will displace the oxygen in the room. Carbon monoxide is said to combine with blood 200 times more easily than oxygen can, so that if you breathe air containing a normal amount of oxygen and a moderate amount of carbon monoxide, your blood will be starved for oxygen. An inadequate supply of oxygen to the brain will result in permanent brain damage or death. The insidious symptoms of carbon monoxide poisoning include drowsiness, headache, flushed complexion, nausea, and vomiting.

You can easily avoid carbon monoxide poisoning if you:

1. Have all heating systems checked annually for operating efficiency. Make sure vents, pipes, and chimneys are tight.

2. Make sure that your heating plant is not starved for air.

3. Make sure that all heating devices designed for venting are properly vented to the outside.

4. Never use hibachis indoors.

5. Never tamper with the ducts or vents of a heating device to produce more heat.

6. Never close your fireplace damper until you are certain that the fire is out.

7. Be sure that the garage is sealed from the house; never run the car in a closed garage.

8. Use your nose to detect the smoke that often accompanies carbon monoxide.

TRANQUILIZERS AND SEDATIVES

It has become popular, even fashionable, for adults to take tranquilizers and sedatives. Physicians are prescribing more and more, while over-the-counter nonprescription drugs also abound. The incidence of accidental ingestion and poisoning with these drugs has also increased. Mothers will often keep tranquilizers or sedatives in their pocketbooks for convenience. One such mother left her purse on the bedroom dresser; one of her children moved it to a chair, within the reach of an even younger child. While the other members of the household were in the living room watching television, the baby removed the box containing the tranquilizers and swallowed the tablets. When his mother returned to the bedroom, she found the child playing with the pocketbook that had contained the tablets. Soon afterward, the child started vomiting, began to cry, and complained of stomach pain. Immediate treatment in a hospital emergency room proved to be lifesaving.

Like aspirin, tranquilizers and sedatives today come in all sizes and shapes and in a multitude of pretty colors, which make them even more enticing and attractive to the child who associates these colors and shapes with candy. Tranquilizers and sedatives should be prescribed only in limited amounts and their containers should have safety closures. If children find them, the difficulty in opening the container and the small amount of medication in it will definitely lessen the chances of an accidental poisoning. Individually packaged tablets in perforated strips are safer and will eliminate a primary cause of accidental childhood poisoning, namely, the uncapped bottle of medication.

ANTIHISTAMINES

For millions of allergic patients throughout this country, antihistamines are common household drugs to be used for the treatment of hay fever and other allergic symptoms. Antihistamines come in a variety of tablets, in multicolored capsules, and in cough mixtures. The side effects, when a child ingests an antihistamine in whatever form, are drowsiness, dizziness, confusion, and inability to coordinate. Associated with these symptoms are dryness of the mouth, nose, and throat. The *immediate treatment for accidental poisoning with antihistamines is elimination of the drug from the body by inducing vomiting*. The child should then be taken to the nearest medical facility for immediate attention and cleansing of the stomach.

What to Do in Case of Poisoning

1. Keep calm—you will act more effectively.
2. Find out what kind of poison was taken and how much by examining the container or any remaining contents.
3. Observe the child's symptoms.
4. Call the doctor, the police, or the poison control center nearest you. Use the list of poison control centers on page 155. **If you cannot reach the poison control center in your area, call the New York number—212-340-4494—which is operative twenty-four hours a day, seven days a week.**
5. Decide whether to induce vomiting. **Vomiting is to be avoided if:**
   (a) The child has swallowed a corrosive poison or petroleum product (see list on page 36). Burns around the mouth may indicate that the child has taken a corrosive poison.
   (b) The child is unconscious or having convulsions.
   (c) The child complains of acute pain.
6. If the child has taken a corrosive or caustic substance, attempt to reduce the absorption of the poison by coating the stomach wall with a demulcent (soothing) substance such as raw egg white or milk. If the skin and clothes are contaminated, flush the skin thoroughly with water and remove the clothes. If the eyes are contaminated, hold the eyelids open and flush with a gentle stream of cool water.
7. If the poison is not corrosive or a petroleum product, induce vomiting by:
   (a) Inserting your finger into the child's throat, or

(b) Administering syrup of ipecac (never with activated charcoal). Two or 3 teaspoonful will cause vomiting within five to fifteen minutes. This dose may be repeated in twenty minutes if vomiting does not occur. You may also use 2 tablespoonsful of salt in a glass of warm water.

8. After the child has vomited, neutralize the poison remaining in his stomach by administering one or two tablespoonsful of activated charcoal USP in 8 ounces of tap water. **Give activated charcoal only after vomiting.**

9. If the child has stopped breathing, administer mouth-to-mouth resuscitation.

(a) Clear the child's mouth with your fingers. Keep his tongue from being swallowed. Place the child on his back, lift his neck, tilt his head back.

(b) Place your mouth tightly over the child's mouth, closing off the nostrils at the same time to prevent the escape of air. The mouth and nose of an infant or young child should be tightly covered by your mouth.

(c) Breathe into the child's mouth or nose until you see his chest rise, then remove your mouth and listen for him to exhale. Repeat, removing your mouth each time to allow the air to escape. For children, small puffs of air repeated about twenty times per minute should be continued until the child breathes for himself.

10. **Rush the child to the nearest hospital.**

CORROSIVE AND PETROLEUM PRODUCTS

Ammonia water
Benzine
Borax
Deodorizers
Detergent powders
Dishwasher granules
Disinfectants
Drain cleaner
Fuel or diesel oil
Gasoline
Household acids
Household bleach
Iodine
Kerosene
Lighter fluid
Lubricating, motor, or
   cutting oil
Naphtha
Pine oil
Rust remover
Toilet bowl cleaner
Transmission fluid
Turpentine
Water softeners

Poison Control Centers

Poison control centers give parents, patients, doctors, and hospitals immediate information about what to do in the event of a poisoning emergency.

To obtain the phone number of the poison control center nearest you, refer to the appendix, pages 155–253.

The first organized attempt to solve the poison control problem was made by doctors who received an increasing number of calls by parents of children who had accidentally swallowed a poisonous household product. Aroused by this apparent increased incidence of poisoning, the American Academy of Pediatrics and the American Public Health Association began establishing poison control centers throughout the country. There are now 500 centers to serve parents and physicians in the United States.

Poison control centers are of two types. The first type is an information center remote from the place of treatment and staffed with trained personnel available to those seeking help twenty-four hours a day. The second type is usually located in a hospital facility; it functions twenty-four hours a day, seven days a week, with a physician always on call.

Poison control centers can be called at any time to obtain information concerning the contents of any products that may be accidentally swallowed. Anyone may phone the center nearest his home to obtain information

lifesaving; however, it is preferable to call
ctor first, and then let him call the center. A
physician can more easily interpret the instructions given
by the center and immediately institute the treatment
necessary.

**If you call a poison control center, you are required
to give the following information:**

1. The commercial name or type of the suspected drug.
2. The manufacturer of the product that has been consumed.
3. The ingredients of the product, which are noted on the container.
4. The age of the child.
5. The amount of substance swallowed and when it was swallowed.
6. The symptoms that the child is exhibiting at the time of discovery.

When the center has been given the essential information, the situation is analyzed, an antidote is suggested if it exists (not every poison has a specific antidote), and immediate treatment measures for the poisoning are given to the caller.

Accidental Poisonings Are Preventable

For a poisoning to occur there must be two components: first, a young child who may be impulsive, overreactive, and accident-prone, with a disciplinary problem resulting from a disturbed parent-child relationship; and second, a hazardous substance. Under certain environmental conditions, the child and the hazardous substance can combine to produce an unexpected poisoning. Dangerous factors in the child's environment that may individually or collectively produce an accident include the time of day, the time of the child's next meal, the accessibility of the dangerous substance, emotional stress in the family, and the parental attitudes toward accident prevention.

There is a general feeling among professionals that careless storage and handling of potentially poisonous substances is a major factor in the accidental poisoning of children. There are other specialists who feel that these accidents are due, rather, to psychological factors, especially to the relationship between a child and his mother. It has been said that an accidental poisoning incident may represent a rebellion against parental authority, or it may be an expression of a child's need for attention or security in a disturbed home environment. Whatever the causes, the only real cure for accidental poisonings is prevention.

Safety Closures

Child-resistant closure caps that adults can open but small children cannot, when properly used, can retard or prevent a youngster's ability to gain access to certain potentially poisonous substances.

In the last decade, such safety closures have been designed and tested in an effort to prevent accidental childhood poisonings. However, these safety closures should not create a false sense of security on the part of the parents since they are not foolproof.

In addition to drugs kept in the medicine cabinet, highly toxic household poisons, such as insecticides, rat poisons, and weed killers, must be packaged in containers with safety closures in order to prevent the accidental swallowing of these products. These safety closures are really *"child-resistant containers"* and are not 100 percent protection from unwanted opening by small children. In the prevention of accidents, there is no substitute for parental vigilance, child guidance, or the safe storage of poisonous products.

Guidelines for Preventing Accidental Poisoning in the Home

1. Lock cabinets containing medicines, especially those that are candy-flavored or colored. Never refer to aspirin or other medicine as "candy" to children. Check for unused drugs and clean your medicine cabinet out regularly.

2. Replace all torn or lost labels from medicine bottles and cover with transparent tape to keep them legible. Be sure all poisons are prominently marked.

3. Never leave prescription medicines, such as tranquilizers, sedatives, hormones, etc., around the house on tables or dressers or in pocketbooks.

4. Never use beer and soft drink bottles to store cleaning fluids, paint thinners, insecticides, or other caustic substances. To a child, a soft-drink bottle means something good to drink. Keep dangerous substances in their original containers with proper labels and safety closures.

5. Never store polishes, waxes, bleaching agents, dry-cleaning fluids, drain cleaners, and ammonia in low cabinets or on shelves that are readily accessible to children. Locked cabinets are the best place for storing solid and liquid poisons if there are children in the home.

6. Make a periodic check of all storage areas in the garage, cellar, or attic for discarded potential poisons that might attract children.

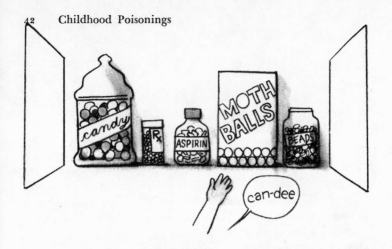

7. Never leave the room, even for a moment, while using a household product that may be a potential poison. Always take the cleaner or polish with you while you answer the door or phone.

8. Never leave a pressurized spray container within easy reach of a child; never dispose of these containers in a furnace or incinerator.

First-Aid Poison Antidote Kit

POWDERED ACTIVATED CHARCOAL

Activated charcoal is an odorless, fine black powder that is the most valuable single antidote and home remedy available today for the immediate treatment of ingested poisons. When given immediately, activated charcoal can absorb large amounts of ingested poison in a short time, thereby giving the parents precious time while waiting for emergency medical care.

The medicine cabinet in every home should contain activated charcoal as a first-aid measure against poisoning. The "little black bottle," as it is often called, is an eye-catcher and a constant reminder to be on the alert against the possible accidental ingestion of poisons in the home.

SYRUP OF IPECAC

Syrup of ipecac should be available in the home in a one-ounce bottle to induce vomiting if necessary in case of poisoning. It is important to remember that one must never use the fluid *extract* of ipecac, since it is fourteen times more powerful than syrup of ipecac and can cause persistent vomiting and diarrhea, sometimes terminating in shock and death. **Be sure to ask your druggist for syrup of ipecac and NOT the fluid extract of ipecac.**

3

Plant Poisoning

Please Don't Eat the Berries

Is there a potentially deadly plant in your home? In your garden? In the neighboring woods? In your favorite picnic area? There are more than 700 species of plant that cause serious illness and even death. Poisonous plants can be found everywhere. Some of the prettiest, which appear innocuous, are potentially poisonous.

To young children some of the green plants, seeds, and flowers may look good enough to eat. The joy of a Christmas season can bring with it the sorrow of an accidental poisoning. Christmas greens such as mistletoe, holly, yew, and Jerusalem cherry, if eaten in large amounts, can cause serious discomfort. It has been stated that one leaf of the flamboyant poinsettia can kill a child. Household pets are also potential victims, the poinsettia being a particularly dangerous one for them as well.

The beautiful larkspur, the attractive lily of the valley, the iris, sweet pea, autumn crocus, and bleeding heart have parts that are toxic if eaten in sufficient amounts. Other common plants such as oleander, wisteria berries, mountain laurel, rhododendron, azalea, yew, and Daphne are potentially toxic and a threat to children.

Plants with small berries are especially dangerous. The seeds of some plants remain in the pod on the vine and present an attractive hazard. The removal of such pods by parents is a desirable safety measure. It must be remembered that certain parts of a plant can be poisonous under certain conditions and harmless under others; and that one part of a plant may be edible while another part may be poisonous.

One summer, one four-year-old child prepared a "luncheon" in the backyard while playing "house." The "lunch" included an apple, a radish, and some berries that she had picked from a nearby shrub. Several hours later, the child collapsed and went into a coma that led to her death. The berries she had eaten were from the Daphne plant. This plant is often cultivated in backyards and also grows wild. In early spring, it has purple-and-white flowers that are followed by small red or yellow berries containing the poison—enough to kill the child who was playing "house."

Another tragedy occurred when a three-year-old child was allowed to play in a vacant lot adjacent to his home, which had been cleared some months earlier in preparation for the construction of a new house. Several large-leafed plants had grown on one side of the lot with drooping clusters of juicy purple berries. When his mother wasn't looking, the child pulled some down and ate them. Their sour taste caused the child to start crying. The mother recognized the fact that the child had eaten the berries because his mouth was stained purple. The child was rushed to a nearby hospital emergency room where efforts to make him vomit the poison berries proved successful. If the amount of berries found in the vomitus had been large, it would have been necessary to pump out his stomach. Fortunately, this was not indicated and the child was sent home.

A case of "mistaken identity" was reported to the New York City Poison Control Center. The incident was reported from rural Connecticut. The reporting physician stated that the patient lived alone and was snowed in. Her daughter had brought her a week's supply of groceries. She also brought a bag of paper white narcissus bulbs. The victim prepared a stew that evening and mistakenly used the flower bulbs in place of onions. About one hour later the woman began vomiting violently and developed colicky cramps and abdominal pains. Medical help was secured and the patient recovered. Because of the marked resemblance of narcissus and other flower bulbs to onions, such incidents as this one are possible and are sometimes fatal. Narcissus, jonquil, and daffodil bulbs should always be stored safely and be kept away from the reach of children.

The U.S. Public Health Service reported that 13,000 persons were victims of plant poisoning in one year, including many fatalities. The statistics also revealed that 12,000 of these were children and that the parents of these youngsters were completely unaware that the surrounding plants eaten were dangerous.

Recognizing and being alert to the possibilities of plant poisoning will help avoid serious trouble. **Be prompt in securing medical help if you suspect a child has eaten parts of the following plants:**

Jimsonweed

JIMSONWEED (STINKWEED OR THORN APPLE)

This plant grows two to five feet tall, has large leaves and funnel-shaped flowers, is found everywhere, and is one of the most common causes of plant poisoning. Children are attracted by the small white flowers that bloom late in the spring. A spinous capsule, which is its fruit, ripens in early fall. All parts of the plant contain poisonous belladonna alkaloids, which have a narcotic effect

Castor Bean

when chewed or brewed. Children who suck the flowers, eat the seeds, or brew "tea" with the leaves have been poisoned while trying it for "kicks" and to get "high." Recognizing and removing this plant is the only way to prevent its ingestion by children.

CASTOR BEANS AND ROSARY PEAS

These beans are especially dangerous to children because they are easily obtainable and very attractive. The rosary pea is a shiny black bean, or sometimes black with red markings. Castor bean seeds are mottled black and brown. These seeds are imported or brought into this

Oleander

country by tourists returning from the Caribbean area. The seeds are used for costume jewelry, such as ornamental necklaces and bracelets. These colorful beads are also frequently used for decoration on purses, gloves, and blouses. The seeds are so toxic that thoroughly chewing just one can kill. These lethal seeds should not be brought into the home in any form.

OLEANDER

This is an evergreen shrub or tree that grows in the South and in California. The twigs, green or dry leaves,

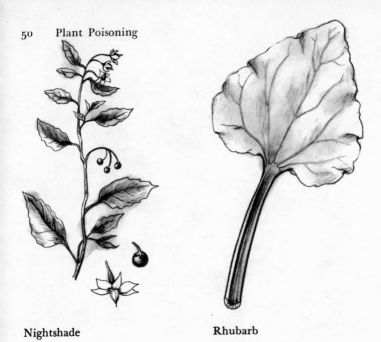

Nightshade   Rhubarb

and flowers of this plant contain a powerful poisonous
substance that can cause death. People have died merely
from eating steaks that were speared with oleander sticks
and roasted over a fire.

NIGHTSHADE (DEADLY NIGHTSHADE)

This family of herbs, shrubs, and trees is found
throughout the United States and contains solanine, a
glycoalkaloid that is highly poisonous in small amounts.

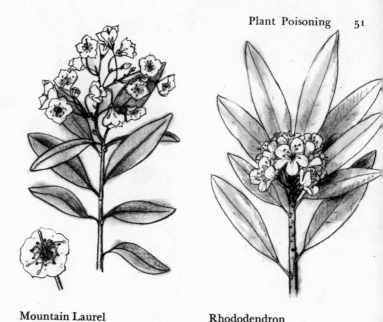

Mountain Laurel   Rhododendron

The common potato is a member of this highly toxic family. All parts of the potato plant, except the tuber, are potentially poisonous.

RHUBARB

The stalk, the part òf this plant that is normally eaten, is harmless. However, the leaf blades or raw leaves contain oxalic acid, which can cause severe kidney damage if eaten uncooked.

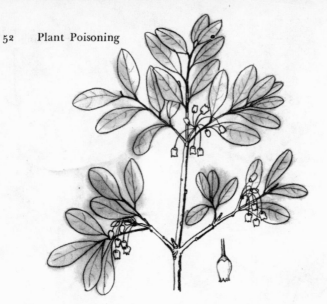

Azalea

Elderberry

Foxglove   Lily of the Valley

MOUNTAIN LAUREL, RHODODENDRON, AND AZALEA

All parts of these common garden plants are poisonous if eaten by children. Children have been poisoned while playing "house" and making "tea" from the leaves and flowers of these plants.

ELDERBERRY

This plant is found in abundance in woods, fields, and picnic areas. The roots, stems, leaves, and unripe berries of the plant can cause an upset stomach, vomiting, and diarrhea.

FOXGLOVE AND LILY OF THE VALLEY

These flowering plants contain a chemical that is a cardiac stimulant. Foxglove is the source of the heart medication called digitalis. Children who eat the tubular flowers, the leaves, or the seeds of the plant are prone to poisoning and heart irregularities.

The problem of poisoning by plants is further complicated by the fact that eating certain parts of everyday fruits and vegetables may be disastrous. *Apple seeds* in large quantities are potentially lethal. *Peach-tree leaves* hold one of the most dangerous poisons known, namely, hydrocyanic acid. The *twigs of cherry trees* release cyanide when chewed, and *elderberries,* considered harmless, have roots that can cause severe nausea and vomiting. In fact, children have been poisoned using elderberry stems for blowguns.

Treatment for Plant Poisoning

Plant poisoning symptoms range from the mild cases associated with nausea and vomiting to the more severe symptoms of coma, convulsions, and death. **Whenever a plant poisoning is suspected, call a doctor immediately** (*see* pages 34–35). The poison control center may be of help if the plant suspected of causing the poison incident can be identified.

In most instances of plant poisoning, the use of syrup of ipecac (*not* extract of ipecac and *not* in conjunction with activated charcoal) to stimulate vomiting can be very helpful in getting rid of the poison in the stomach. However, there are poisonings that do not call for vomiting—poisonings from strong alkaloids and acids. In these cases, vomiting would be injurious to the digestive tract. Phone the poison control center for immediate information as to whether vomiting should be induced or not.

To prevent plant poisonings, the following recommendations may prove helpful:

1. Learn to recognize the plant villains and eradicate them.

2. Keep small children *away* from plants—keep plants *away* from small children.

3. Teach children not to chew on anything other than food.

4. Keep close watch on the little ones in the hand-to-mouth stage, especially when in the garden and in picnic areas, as well as at home.

4

Other Dangerous Drugs

METHADONE (DOLLY)

It is estimated that 15,000 persons in the New York area alone use methadone. This drug is given to heroin addicts as a means of decreasing their craving for heroin. The drug is given as a tablet or dissolved in some type of soft drink. In persons who are gradually given the drug, a tolerance develops that prevents any oversedation, euphoria, or respiratory problems. However, in those individuals who are not tolerant, especially children who may accidentally ingest even small amounts of the drug, the result may be fatal.

Many of the cases of accidental methadone poisoning have been reported in children less than seven years of age. The drug is available in homes and on the street. Children can discover and accidentally swallow methadone tablets that parents, friends, or baby-sitters obtain by prescription and through other sources. Children have secured the drug from parents' handbags or from the tops of sinks, from open cabinets, and from tabletops.

The child who ingests an unknown quantity of methadone by accident becomes comatose and needs immediate treatment. He should be taken to the nearest hospital emergency room with the information that he has ingested methadone. Specific antidotes are available that are lifesaving and must be used by a physician. **Time is of the essence. The victim of accidental methadone ingestion or overdosage must be treated immediately if his life is to be saved.**

LSD (ACID, SUGAR, TRIPS)

Hallucinogenic drugs may be encountered as homemade capsules, powders, or liquids commonly found in the household of the addict. Widespread experimentation with mind-expanding drugs and hallucinogenic agents has increased the possibility that younger siblings in the household may be exposed to and accidentally ingest these substances.

One recent victim was a five-year-old girl who became acutely ill and psychotic following a single accidental ingestion of LSD. On arising one morning, this child began to make breakfast for herself and her younger brother— the custom in the household was for the children to help themselves while the adults slept late. She used a sugar tablet that she found in the refrigerator. Within fifteen minutes, she began to scream and cry, creating a commotion that aroused the other members of the household. It was subsequently revealed that the sugar tablet had contained LSD. It belonged to her eighteen-year-old brother who had stored it in the refrigerator for future use.

The ingestion of LSD produces reactions that can be harmful and dangerous. Hallucinogenic drugs cause the user's mind to wander in a dreamy state, and objects, time, and place are not clearly delineated. The hallucinations may last for days and may recur without further drug ingestion. Homicidal and suicidal impulses may become apparent. Permanence of mental derangement is questionable, although damage to chromosomes, and hence to offspring, has been demonstrated.

MARIJUANA (POT, GRASS, TEA)

There are many reasons why youngsters "turn on" to drugs. Those most commonly expressed include the attraction of a thrill, the danger involved in "pleasure seeking," and the gaining of status with peers by "keeping up with the crowd." Youngsters are usually introduced to drugs by friends who are themselves drug users. This type of peer pressure is the most important single factor in encouraging juvenile experimentation with drugs. Marijuana can be smoked, swallowed, or sniffed, and it can cause stimulation, depression, or hallucinations. The symptoms produced are dependent upon the quantity and quality of the material used and the personality of the individual user.

Because of vivid visions and euphoria, excessive use or an accidental overdose can cause the user to lose all restraint and act in a violent manner. Marijuana users may feel exhilarated or relaxed, stare off into space, be hilarious without apparent cause, and take on an exaggerated sense of their capabilities. The use of marijuana can also promote accident-proneness and alterations of the senses of time and space.

Parents may discover that their children have been using marijuana when they detect its distinctive, sweetish odor. Marijuana users often employ incense to mask this odor.

HEROIN (JUNK, HORSE, BAG)

Heroin is a powerfully addictive derivative of opium, white in color and resembling powdered sugar. Heroin is usually "sniffed" by teen-agers who are unaware of the dangers of the drug. Actually heroin can pass through the nasal mucous membranes into the bloodstream and anyone with a sensitivity to the drug can suffer a deadly reaction. The drug can be injected into the skin ("skin popping") or into a vein ("mainlining").

If you suspect that your child is experimenting with heroin because of a marked change in his behavior, the following are some physical signs worth noting.

The abuser can be spotted by constricted pupils and a calm, inattentive appearance. Heroin users usually experience an unusual appetite for sweets. In addition, parents may come upon such paraphernalia as hypodermic syringes, bent spoons, and pieces of rubber tubing.

A slow pulse and respiration are characteristic of heroin addiction. Youngsters are very sensitive to the depressant respiratory effects until tolerance develops. Psychic and physical dependency develop readily with a characteristic withdrawal syndrome. **If a parent suspects that a child is suffering from an overdose of heroin, emergency medical treatment in the nearest hospital may be lifesaving.** Convulsions and deaths from accidental overdoses are reported daily.

AMPHETAMINES (BENNIES, DEXIES, SPEED, PEP PILLS)

Amphetamines are stimulants that come in multicolored capsules. They are often prescribed by physicians for appetite control and weight reduction. The drug is also often used to relieve mental depression, control wakefulness, and increase energy. A normal dose of the drug produces an increased alertness, a feeling of increased initiative, and an almost abnormal cheerfulness, along with the ability to go without sleep for prolonged periods of time. Amphetamines, however, can cause high blood pressure, heart irregularities, and heart attacks. Highway accidents have been attributed to the driver's loss of control resulting from the use of amphetamines.

After prolonged usage, amphetamines have definite effects on the body, causing the individual to sweat excessively and become jittery; they also produce confusion, diarrhea, enlargement of the pupils, a fast heart rate, hallucinations, loss of appetite, and a dangerous aggressiveness.

Teen-agers often take these pills to increase their "nerve" and as a result may behave dangerously. If overdosed, the individual will suffer side effects that can lead to death. The abuser of amphetamines can be spotted by his restlessness, nervousness, hand tremors, dilated pupils, and heavy breathing. The juvenile may be talkative and have delusions, hallucinations, or exhibit signs of psychosis. **Parents noting these symptoms in youngsters and having reason to suspect that they have taken an overdose of amphetamine drugs should seek out emergency medical care in the nearest hospital emergency room or physician's office.** Time is of the essence if medical treatment is to be successful.

ASTHMA POWDERS

Asthma powders, originally meant for inhaling by asthmatic patients, are being used today by young people experimenting with drugs as a means of producing euphoria, or a "high." Taken by mouth rather than inhaled, asthma powders are popular with young people because of their availability owing to a lack of legal restrictions on their sale. Unfortunately, in one year five deaths were reported to have occurred due to the impairment of judgment and physical coordination secondary to the effects of these asthma powders.

Warning Signs of Drug Abuse

Youngsters may find themselves in situations where narcotics and other dangerous substances are available and being urged upon them. Parents should be aware of this possibility and instruct their children on the dangers of drug abuse and the deadly effects of overdosage.

Parents should check for these common symptoms in children if drug usage is suspected:

1. A change in work or school attendance, deportment, or grades.

Drug Paraphernalia

2. An unusual frequency of outbreaks of temper.

3. Poor physical appearance.

4. Wearing of sunglasses at inappropriate times to hide dilated or constricted pupils.

5. Long-sleeved shirts worn constantly to hide needle marks.

6. Change in the character of work accomplished.

7. Disappearance of clothing and personal belongings from the home.

8. Association with known drug users and rejection of old friends.

9. Spending unusual amounts of time in locked bathrooms.

10. Being found during the day in odd places such as closets, storage rooms, and other isolated areas where drugs might be taken.

5

Automobile Accidents

The automobile has brought the American people a way of life and enjoyment, but it has also brought with it misery, injury, and death. Today the motor vehicle, more than ever, poses a great threat to young lives. According to the American Medical Association, automobile accidents are one of the major unsolved health problems. This can be verified by the tragic and staggering statistics indicating the important role that accidental deaths and injury due to automobiles play in this country. In 1967 more children aged one to fourteen years died in automobile accidents than died of meningitis, heart disease, pneumonia, and congenital malformations combined. Automobile accidents outrank, ten to one, all crimes of violence in the United States. In 1969 an estimated 258,-000 children were injured and 5,591 were killed while passengers in autos.

There are a number of high-risk situations in which children are most exposed to accidental injury. These include riding in a car without the benefit of seatbelts or other safety devices, using a school bus, and playing in a driveway. Children injured in automobile accidents appear to fall into certain action patterns: coming from between parked cars, playing in the street or driveway, or crossing an intersection against the traffic light.

A lack of seatbelts contributed to almost 16,000 instances of facial and dental injuries among children in a recent one-year period. Pupils using school buses face the growing risk of being involved in traffic accidents. Statistics compiled by the National Safety Council indicate that 3,700 children were injured and fifty were killed in school bus accidents in 1965. Those who were injured or killed incurred head or chest injuries from striking seat arms or backs, the unpadded sides of buses, or sharp objects such as fire extinguishers and even heaters. Another high-risk situation involves the young child playing in a driveway—a uniquely hazardous area. About 300 children under five years of age died in 1972 when struck by automobiles in driveways, most of them driveways of their own homes.

Automobile accidents involving young people are on the increase for a number of reasons. Children today learn about cars early and try to be the first with the best, most powerful, smartest, and fastest automobile while engaging in the more dangerous risk-taking experiences. All this with little thought given to their safety or the safety of others.

The recent youth involvement with drug experimentation has increased the young person's potential for harming himself and others. Whether the youngster uses marijuana, pep pills, sedatives, or mind-expanding drugs, the results are the same. There is a distortion of perception and judgment that increases the possibility of accidental injury or death. Educators, medical men, and social agencies have expressed great concern for the problem of drug abuse by young people as it contributes to vehicular accidents.

Moreover, drugs that are prescribed to adults to relieve their pain, tension, or anxiety can impair their reactions as well. For example, there is the case of the mother who takes a tranquilizer to calm her nerves and simultaneously a decongestant to soothe her aching sinuses. An hour later she picks up her children from school. On the way home she becomes very sleepy and finds it difficult to keep the car on the right side of the road. The drive is a nightmare in which she barely misses other cars. This housewife certainly did not recognize the fact that the drugs she was taking had undesirable side effects and could have jeopardized the well-being of her children as well as her own.

In addition to drugs, other factors such as fatigue, worry, illness, anger, tension, and alcohol all contribute to the incidence of automobile accidents.

Another young mother piles the children into the car and drives off to the shopping center. The children bounce and jump on the seat; they climb from the front seat to the back, distracting their mother. These children are being exposed to an unnecessary risk by being allowed to move around in a moving car. If a crash occurred, they would be thrown from the car or hurled like missiles against the windshield.

It has been clearly demonstrated that passengers wearing seatbelts sustain fewer injuries and have a much higher survival rate than those who are not so protected. The child without a seatbelt is often a victim of injuries during a sudden, jolting stop in traffic, while the child who is buckled in does not interfere with or distract the driver.

Currently available information indicates that if all passengers used seatbelts at all times, 8,000 to 10,000 lives would be saved annually. However, surveys have revealed that seatbelts are used only about 40 percent of the time, on the average. Fewer than 20 percent of the parents questioned locked car doors before starting the engine, seated children in the rear, or used any type of safety belt when traveling with their children in automobiles.

One pediatrician recently stated: "Child restraints are to auto accidents what immunizations are to diseases." However, the type of restraint used must be suitable, adequate, and effective. Standard seatbelts are simply not suitable for infants or small children. In fact, standard seatbelts made for adults have actually contributed to some injuries to children. In addition, the car seats previously sold for children's use have been found to be entirely unsatisfactory and have increased rather than decreased the risks of accidental injury. Parents should buy devices labeled as meeting the specifications of the motor vehicle safety standards introduced in April, 1971. Children's car seats manufactured prior to April, 1971, do not meet the safety standards. Parents may feel secure if they buy car seats and harnesses labeled as meeting Federal Motor Vehicle Safety Standard No. 213 for car seats and No. 209, Type 3, for harnesses.

The American Academy of Pediatrics Committee on Accident Prevention has issued recommendations for the proper use of safety devices for infants and children traveling in cars. They have emphatically stated that the child's size and weight determines the appropriate type of auto safety restraint for him.

Up to about six months of age, the baby should be put in a firmly constructed, well-padded car bed, usually in the rear of the car and securely fastened with a seatbelt to the car structure. The axis of the car bed should be parallel to that of the automobile. *Never* hold the baby while you are riding even if you are sitting in the back. In a collision the baby might be hurled against the interior of the car or thrown out. *Never* allow an infant or child on the front seat because of the greater risk of the infant's striking the dashboard or the windshield. *Never* use the type of child's seat that merely rests on a seat or hooks on the back since this type of device offers no protection to the child at all.

Children weighing less than 50 pounds should be restrained by a harness or one of the new children's safety seats. If a small child is hyperactive and cannot remain seated for any length of time, he may be made comfortable in a children's harness that is attached to the body of the car or is used in conjunction with a seatbelt. Harnesses of this type made within the safety standard requirements allow a child to stand up, lie down, or move about within a very limited area. *These harnesses are too large to provide protection for infants and small children and should not be used for them.*

Child seating systems have been devised for safety and are offered for sale as effective restraints. However, their effectiveness depends on understanding and following the instructions for usage.

Both Ford and General Motors have available specially designed safety seats for young children. The Ford seat, called "Tot-Guard," consists of a polyethylene shield. The pad and shield are slipped over the youngster's legs and body with the regular car seat buckling around the child, holding him securely in place but allowing him some room for wiggling.

Basket for Child up to Six Months of Age

Harness and Safety Seat for Child up to Fifty Pounds

The General Motors child seat is made from molded
plastic and has a padded rail that lifts up like the tray
of a high chair, making it easy for a child to slip in and
out of the seat. A strap buckles around the youngster's
chest and the child and seat are fastened with the stand-

Lap Belt for Child over Five Years of Age

ard seatbelt. This model is easy to install and remove
and can be used in any standard car that is fitted with
seatbelts. When not in use, the seat can be easily folded
and stored.

Children over five years of age can use a standard lap
belt for safety. The child can be placed over a hard
cushion with the lap belt securely fastened. This type
of "booster" cushion elevates the child and enlarges his
range of vision, thereby avoiding the temptation of
wearing the belt loosely.

The simple lap belt for older children is considered
by some safety experts to be incomplete and inadequate
protection. Potential injury could be lessened by having
the older child wear a three-point combined lap and
shoulder belt.

Remember: Just as you would take your child to a
pediatrician to immunize him against infections, immunize him against motor vehicle accident injury by using

an adequate, safe seat restraint correct for his weight and size. It may be your child's life that is saved.

To sum up, the sad statistics concerning automobile accidents can be lessened if all individuals occupying a vehicle follow basic safety rules. The burden of carrying out these rules falls on parents, both by means of the example they set while driving and by means of the instructions they give their children on safety—always supplemented by a firm and consistent discipline.

Safety Rules of the Road for Children

1. Children should always enter an automobile on the side opposite the driver, namely, the right side.

2. Children should keep their fingers away from car doors. One of the most painful and frequent childhood injuries is a finger pinched in a closing car door.

3. Adults should get out of cars before children at all times.

4. Children should never be permitted to stand next to the driver or stand on a car seat in a moving vehicle.

5. Never allow a child to lie on the shelf behind the back seat.

6. Lock all doors before starting the car.

7. Fasten all safety restraints securely.

8. Never permit children to toss around objects such as toys, pillows, or other playthings inside a moving car.

9. Never seat a child on the driver's lap.

10. Teach children to keep their hands off the controls and the dashboard.

11. Never leave a child alone in a parked car.

12. Always carry a first-aid kit in order to manage minor cuts and abrasions that children commonly encounter.

13. Always have available fresh batteries, a flashlight, and an emergency spotlight to alert other drivers in case of an accident.

14. Teach your child to look in all directions before crossing the street.

15. Teach him to cross streets only at marked crosswalks or intersections.

16. Carefully explain to him the dangers of running into the street, running out from behind parked cars, or jaywalking.

17. Teach your child how to read traffic lights, highway signs, and signals.

What to Do in Case of an Automobile Accident

1. Protect your car from further accidents by waving oncoming cars past.

2. Ask someone to call the police immediately.

3. Comfort the injured, but do not move them until a doctor, ambulance, or the police arrive.

4. If a child or adult is trapped but can easily be released, do so without tugging.

5. *In case of severe bleeding* apply a tourniquet at the site of the bleeding. *If the blood is gushing* from a deep wound, apply a pressure dressing with a folded cloth. Always keep the patient warm until medical help arrives.

6. Always use a flashing police-type light to warn off oncoming cars. Always keep one of these in your car in case of emergency.

7. Avoid the use of light flares near the car and permit no one to smoke—there may be a posibility of fire or explosion.

6
Bicycles and Boats

Bicycle Accidents

With the dramatic upsurge in the popularity of bicycle riding in the last decade there has been a corresponding increase in bike-related injuries, especially to children. All the statistics of bicycling in the United States appear to be on the increase: the number of bicycles, riders, bicycle thefts, and cyclists' injuries.

Bicycle accidents account for one-third of all nonpassenger traffic injuries to children between the ages of five and fifteen. About 80 percent of the injuries suffered by bike-riding youngsters occur in urban areas. Today, bicycles are responsible for an estimated 1 million injuries annually, including 120,000 fractures and 60,000 concussions. Collisions between bicycles and automobiles produce 34,000 injuries annually. The deaths from these collisions began to exceed 800 a year five years ago. Another forty-five to eighty deaths annually are the result of bicycle mishaps that do not involve motor vehicles.

Recently designed bicycles, particularly the unstable

high-risers, cause more serious injuries than other bikes. Such bikes require greater skill to operate, are less stable and harder to steer, and thereby contribute to a variety of injuries. Injuries to the head, face, and genital area are more common among children riding the high-rise bicycles. Genital injuries are inflicted by gear-shift levers that protrude from the horizontal crossbar. Another factor contributing to accidental injury with bicycles is that some children ride bicycles that are too big for them.

Parents are faced with the problem of purchasing the proper type of bicycle for their child. They must decide whether a child is able to handle a regular or a high-rise bike. Not much is known about how or when children develop bike-riding skills. However, high-rise bicycles are not recommended for beginning riders. These bikes do not balance easily and most learners feel rather uncomfortable using them. If a child appears well coordinated for his age and has no trouble riding a conventional bike, the age of nine with at least three years of riding experience is probably the safest time for a high-rise. Younger riders are safer on bikes with coaster brakes. Hand brakes take more coordination and until about the age of eleven, youngsters may be more confused than helped by hand brakes. After the age of eleven, most children have the coordination necessary to work the hand brakes well enough to benefit from their superior stopping power.

If parents select a bike of the right size that does not demand more skill than the child has, the risk of a really serious accident can be reduced.

Parents should only consider purchasing a bicycle for their child under the following circumstances:

1. He is old enough to keep the bike in good shape.
2. There are safe places to ride a bike near his home, such as bicycle paths and other marked areas.
3. He lives in a safe area not heavily congested with traffic.
4. He gets proper instruction in bicycle safety before he is permitted to ride in traffic.

When buying a child's bicycle, avoid hand brakes that are too large for small hands, gear shifts mounted too far back, a "sissy bar" protruding behind the seat that makes dismounting difficult, and a small front wheel that makes the bike hard to steer. Be sure that the bicycle is equipped for maximum safety with headlight, taillight, warning bell, chain guard, and coaster brake.

Last, but not least, your child must be given respon-
sibilities. He must meet them and you must see that he
does. Many children would be spared bike injuries if
their parents took the time to teach common-sense rules
of the road.

Children's Rules of the Road for Safe Cycling

1. Keep to the extreme right of the road.
2. Always come to a full stop and look in each direction before entering any main streets and highways.
3. Ride in single file at all times.
4. Never stunt-ride.
5. Never ride on ice or snow.
6. Do not carry passengers.
7. Do not hitch rides.
8. Wear light-colored clothing when riding at night.
9. Have a headlight, a rear reflector, and pedals with built-in reflectors on the bicycle.
10. Be sure brakes are in good condition.
11. Use a rack or basket for packages.
12. Have a bell or horn on the bicycle.
13. Use a guard clip on trouser cuffs.
14. Oil or grease working parts as necessary.
15. Keep all nuts or screws tight and check them at periodic intervals.
16. Keep tires properly inflated.
17. Keep well back from moving cars—they might stop suddenly.
18. Be alert for pedestrians who might step from between parked cars.
19. Avoid driving too fast downhill or on rough, slippery roads.

Remember: A bicycle driven in a traffic area is a traffic vehicle and subject to the same laws, highway signs and traffic-control signals as motor vehicles. Bicycles in traffic are just like automobiles. A cyclist must stop for traffic lights and stop signs, give hand signals, and ride on the right side of the street. Failure to do so is against the law.

The Child as a Bicycle Passenger

Children as bicycle passengers pose a real hazard and add to the number of needlessly inflicted accidental bike injuries. The child who rides as a passenger on a bicycle built for one often entangles a foot between the frame and the wheel spokes. A study was made of fourteen bicycle-spoke injuries and it was noted that victims were riding as passengers on rear fenders, handlebars, and crossbars with no safety precautions observed for the legs and feet.

With the present level of bicycle usage in this country, the possibility of bicycle-spoke injuries to a passenger is a very real one. The injuries resulting can range from a minor abrasion to sprains or severe lacerations. Frequently, fractures of the foot and ankle result from accidents in which a child's foot is caught in the spokes of a bicycle.

Both riders on a bicycle built for one are endangered because of the problems of stability, distracting activity, and the possibility of a collision or a fall being precipitated by the passenger's foot being caught in the spokes.

If children are to be passengers, it is essential that they ride in an appropriate child carrier. Several models are available. All have seatbelts or lap restraints and those intended for installation over the fenders have shields guarding the legs and feet from the spokes. Ideally, these carriers should have straps to prevent the child's feet from slipping away from the shields and dangling near the wheels.

Minibikes Are Not Toys

The minibike, cause of many unfortunate accidents, is enjoying increasing popularity among teen-agers. A small motorcycle with a top speed of 30 to 40 miles per hour, the minibike is designed for the five-to-eight-year-old youngster and is usually loaded with all kinds of hardware. The riders of these bicycles are subject to many of the hazards that make the motorcycle widely known as the most dangerous machine on wheels. As many as 3 to 4 million minibikes are in use, whether or not they are legal or safe. After mastering the backyard or the driveway, youngsters are likely to end up in the open spaces of a shopping mall or parking lot where they become prime candidates for serious accidents.

Minibikes are dangerous. Those using a bike of this type should wear a helmet at all times since most of the serious accidents to riders involve head injuries. Other safety suggestions include: wear shatterproof goggles or a face shield; no double riding; no street riding; no tricky steering; and avoid riding on loose gravel or on wet or slippery pavement.

It is illegal to ride minibikes on any public highway unless they are properly equipped and the rider has a license. When a driver's license is granted, the rules are the same as for the usage of motorcycles. Riders must meet the minimum age requirement. If an unlicensed youngster is found riding one of these vehicles, his parents can be subject to a fine in some states.

Skateboarding

A sport fad called skateboarding or sidewalk surfing has captured the enthusiasm of millions of young children and teen-agers. It involves the use of a small wooden or plastic board about 2 feet long and 6 inches wide with movable roller-skate–type wheels attached on the bottom, two on each side. Skateboarding requires many of the same athletic skills as surfing and skating. An accomplished performer can do an amazing variety of stunts. On the other hand, most tragically, youngsters have been killed in skateboard collisions with automobiles. In a single month in a New York hospital, doctors treated fifty young victims of skateboarding accidents in a community of 82,000. The frequency of these accidents is convincing proof that skateboards do constitute a safety hazard unless the rider exercises considerable caution.

SKATEBOARDING SAFETY RULES

1. Do not skateboard on public streets or on driveways that incline into the street.
2. Use only paved surfaces free of large bumps and cracks that cause spills.
3. Wear sneakers or shoes with nonslip soles.
4. Emphasize control of the skateboard, not speed.
5. Be sure that the skateboard is not broken or cracked and that the wheel mechanisms are not loose.

Boating Accidents

In the year 1970, there were 3,803 boating accidents reported involving some 4,762 vessels. Over half the accidents reported involved collisions, which accounted for many of the personal injuries. Fires and explosions resulted in the second largest number of injuries. In the same year, the Coast Guard reported 1,305 drowning victims, 47.2 percent of whom were known to have had lifesaving devices available. However, 81.7 percent of these victims did not use the devices or used them improperly and 20.7 percent of the drowning victims were known not to have had lifesaving devices available.

Each year, more and more boating enthusiasts enjoy

one of the country's fastest-growing recreational activities. Unfortunately, with its joy and relaxation comes the fact that a serious accident problem has been created.

In boating, just as in driving a car, certain basic safe operating practices must be followed. They must be learned and they must be mastered if boating pleasure is to be pleasure and not to result in an unfortunate tragedy.

BOATING SAFETY RULES

1. Boating is no fun in bad weather and can be extremely hazardous. Always check the weather forecast before getting underway and stay ashore if any of the radio or television signals indicate poor weather conditions.

2. Don't try to tow a water skier alone. You just can't watch ahead and watch the skier at the same time. Before you try to tow a water skier, make sure you have the feel of your boat; that is, how it makes turns and how quickly it stops when the engine is stopped. It will feel different when you are towing a skier.

3. Keep an approved fire extinguisher aboard.

4. Never sit on the bow of a small boat. Lives are lost when children fall overboard with a sudden turn of the boat or a sudden slowing and then speeding up of the motor.

5. Never overload your boat. A major cause of drowning in boating accidents is the overturning or overloading of boats.

6. Always carry a life preserver for each person aboard and be sure that children wear life preservers at all times when on the boat.

If someone falls in the water toss him a life preserver or life jacket if available, or anything that will float such as a beach ball, the inner tube of a tire, or a chunk of wood. Extend a fishing pole, oar, or any long object that is handy to him and pull him to the boat.

7

Machinery-Related Accidents

The Lawn Mower

The rotary-power lawn mower is probably the most dangerous piece of machinery that can be found around the home and has become a leading cause of accidents. The latest U.S. Public Health Service statistics indicate that power mowers may cause more than 140,000 injuries annually.

Unfortunately, the rotary mower's threat of severe injury's happening faster than the wink of an eye can make a simple lawn mowing a hazardous experience—and children are often the victims. A high proportion of lawn-mower accidents, 20 to 30 percent, occur among children under the age of thirteen.

One six-year-old girl suffered a skull fracture from a stone that struck her head while her father was mowing the lawn. A twelve-year-old was hit on the leg by another missile, lacerating the muscles. A four-year-old boy entered the emergency room with a metal rod protruding from his head as a result of a rotary mower accident. A

four-year-old boy was riding on the back of a mower driven by his grandfather when he suddenly jumped off and caught his clothing in the machinery. The mower cut off the heel of the boy's boot and just missed his foot.

Young children should never be permitted to operate a riding power lawn mower. One seven-year-old boy had the end of his index finger amputated while attempting to clear the blade. A twelve-year-old boy suffered severe burns when gas he had spilled on the mower ignited, causing the tank to blow up. A two-year-old was playing nearby while his mother mowed the lawn. He suddenly reached down, touched the twirling blade, and lost the tip of one finger.

Children shouldn't even be in the yard when grass is being cut with a rotary mower. The rotating blade can make a lethal missile of a stone or a small piece of wood. A young child shouldn't be allowed to handle any hazardous machinery, particularly the rotary lawn mower. A child doesn't have the safety knowledge nor the experience that these deadly machines require.

The primary rule for safety is to buy the safest mower. It must be well designed and have good balance. The rotating parts must be covered with built-in guards, and the side should be enclosed with strong guards. The handle should be long enough to keep the machine well away from one's feet.

SAFETY RULES TO BE FOLLOWED WHEN USING A LAWN MOWER

1. Never try to adjust or repair the machine while the motor is running.
2. Before cutting the lawn, thoroughly rake it to remove twigs, stones, toys, and other solid objects, no matter how small.
3. Periodically clean and inspect the motor to make sure all nuts and bolts are tight.
4. Don't allow children to use the power mower.
5. Never cut wet grass with an electric mower.
6. Never reach under the mower to lift or tip it.
7. Keep the speed of the mower low enough so that you can control it; don't allow the machine to pull you.
8. Don't refuel the mower while it is hot.
9. Never leave the mower running unattended.

10. Avoid wearing inappropriate clothing such as a tie, long-sleeved shirt, apron, loose pants, scarf, or the like that could become entangled in the moving parts.

Garage-Door Accidents

Electronically operated roll-up garage doors have caused critical injuries to children because some have faulty controls and can be activated accidentally. In one case, a group of children were playing a game that required that each one run out of the garage before the electronically operated door closed. A five-year-old boy did not make it, was struck on the neck, and killed instantly. In another case, a rope attached to the garage door became entangled around a child's neck and she was elevated off the ground and strangled. These are just a few of the garage-door accidents that can occur.

To prevent such injuries, homeowners should install the new safety electronic doors that stop automatically and reverse if they come in contact with a solid object. Garage doors can be made safe by keeping them closed at all times and never allowing children to play with them. Danger could be further avoided by ordinances and state laws that would not permit any garage door to be installed without a fully automatic reversible mechanism.

Escalator Amputations

A pleasant day of shopping in a department store can turn into a nightmare. One three-year-old boy's hand was seriously injured as it became caught in the metal meshing of the store's escalator when his mother was not watching him. Physicians have coined the term "escalator amputation" to describe the not infrequent occurrence wherein children lose or damage fingers and toes while riding on escalators.

Children should never be allowed to ride barefoot on escalators, and children in strollers should *never* be put on escalators. Parents should always hold small children securely in their arms, and hold older children by the hand when ascending or descending on an escalator. The end of the stairs is a frightening experience for a child who finds himself falling hands first into the disappearing steps of the escalator.

Instantaneous Washday Amputations

The innocent-looking washing machine with its spin dryer poses an exceedingly serious hazard to the child.

Children have lost limbs while playing with a top-loading washing machine that was going through its high-speed damp-dry cycle.

In some areas of the country, the old-fashioned clothes wringer has not been replaced by the automatic washer-dryer. The wringer is another definite hazard to a child's upper extremities. Medical reports describe inquisitive, impulsive youngsters who have reached into a clothes wringer, incurring serious injury and possible amputation of their hands. Awareness on the part of the parents can help avoid this type of injury.

Other case histories illustrate mishaps to children when machines have not been stopped before opening. Fortunately, today's home washing machines have switches that automatically cut off power when the lid is opened. Only through such reliable safety devices can some of these tragic accidents to children's limbs be prevented. Parents must be aware that a serious hazard exists in a seemingly innocent home appliance.

Refrigerator Suffocations

Each year a number of young children perish as a result of being locked in ice boxes, refrigerators, and freezers. These children's deaths are appalling since they suffocate needlessly. Empty refrigerators appeal to children between three and six years of age as attractive places in which to play. Some children use abandoned and open refrigerators as hiding places.

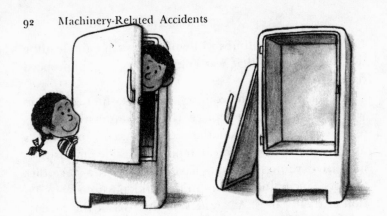

Children enter refrigerators singly or in groups—a number of instances are recorded in which one or more children were fatally trapped in a refrigerator during play. Occasionally a child may be pushed into the refrigerator by another child who wishes to scare him. If he is trapped, there is enough air in the refrigerator to keep a child alive for only ten to fifteen minutes.

Children may enter refrigerators that have been abandoned in dumps, but many are trapped in temporarily empty refrigerators in homes or in vacant apartments. If a refrigerator, ice box, or freezer stands empty and idle for a period of time, it becomes a menace to the life of a child.

HOW TO CHILDPROOF A REFRIGERATOR

1. If you plan to abandon, discard, or junk a refrigerator, remove the door completely.

2. Have the appliance carted away and destroyed as quickly as possible. Don't leave it around your home or grounds where it becomes a hazard to playing children.

3. If you are disposing of a refrigerator that still has its door, place the unit, if it is an upright one, so that the door is facing the wall. Or lock the door with a padlock—an ordinary chain wrapped around the box can be secured with a padlock. The door may also be secured with self-adhesive filament tape.

4. An extra precaution, in addition to whatever method you use to secure the door so that it won't open, is to leave the shelves of your refrigerator in to discourage a child who may be tempted to climb in if he finds the cabinet empty.

In addition to making your refrigerator childproof, teach your child what he needs to know about refrigerators, ice boxes, and home freezers. He should be taught to stay away from them because they are not playthings. He must be warned that if by accident he does get caught inside a refrigerator no one will hear him if he cries, nor can he be seen, nor will he be able to breathe. The older child should be instructed on how to help a younger child found playing in a refrigerator. He should waste no time in helping the younger child out immediately. Then he should report to his parents the presence of a discarded refrigerator, home freezer, or ice box that poses a danger and is a deadly toy to the unsuspecting child at play.

8

Toys Can Be Dangerous

Every year, 700,000 unfortunate youngsters suffer injuries while playing with toys. These colorful, attractive playthings can be lethally dangerous. One eight-year-old child's face was burned beyond recognition when the hair of a highly flammable doll she was playing with caught fire. A six-year-old boy looked down the barrel of his dart gun to see why the darts did not come out; suddenly, a dart escaped, causing an eye injury that led to blindness. A seven-year-old boy could hardly wait to use his new dart set. His four-year-old brother raced after him to the family garage to tack up a small bull's-eye target. The older boy, anxious to start, began throwing darts without noticing that his brother was in the target's path. A six-inch-long dart with its needle-sharp point penetrated the youngster's eye. A year-old infant was given a musical toy for his crib. The father suspended it from two small strings, stretched from either side of the crib, so that the baby could reach it for play. Left alone for a few minutes, the active child accidentally tangled the cord around his neck and choked to death.

Despite major strides by American manufacturers to insure toy safety, unsafe toys are still available, and major injuries and fatalities can be traced to their faulty construction. Rag dolls are constructed with dangerously sharp wires. Cuddly dogs or dolls are manufactured with sharp-pointed metal objects embedded in their eyes that can easily be loosened and swallowed by a child. Space rockets are sold with sharp, unyielding metal fins that can easily slash a child's flesh. The poor stitching on stuffed toys often allows potentially hazardous flammable and contaminated material to escape from the toy.

Dangerous projectile toys are sold to children as young as six years old. Kids like them and suffer because of them. The National Society for the Prevention of Blindness recently reported that 17 percent of the 160 eye injuries suffered each year by school-age children are caused by missile-type playthings. Missile toys include bows and arrows, air guns, peashooters, slingshots, darts, and guns that shoot darts or plastic pellets.

If you must buy a missile toy for your child:

    1. Be sure your child is mature enough to understand the risks associated with this type of toy and willing to take the necessary safety precautions.

    2. Teach him how to use the toy. Stay and observe him while he is learning.

    3. Provide him with a suitable area in which to use his missile toy.

    4. Remember that younger children in the family may wander into the area where the older child is using a missile toy.

It is the responsibility of parents to buy the right toy for the right child at the right time. Toys that are brought into the home must be safe for the age of the children they are given to. Many children are hurt each year playing with toys they are not ready for. The type of toy must

measure up to the age and size of the child. It should also suit the child's personality. If a child has a tendency to throw things, make sure his toys are soft and pliable. If he is fond of taking things apart, make sure his toys are not difficult to take apart or he will hurt himself.

Toy Safety

1. *When buying toys for children, follow these suggestions to prevent accidental injury and perhaps death:*
   a. Check the age group for which the toy is intended.
   b. Check fabrics for flammability.
   c. Avoid buying projectile toys—they pose a high risk of accident.
   d. Avoid toys with detachable parts that can be swallowed or placed in the ear or nose.
   e. Avoid toys made of lead or colored with lead-base paint that could expose a curious, nibbling infant to lead poisoning.
   f. Avoid giving a child under twelve years of age any electrical toy such as an imitation electric stove or iron, since they can cause serious burns or electric shock.

2. *Toys for infants or young children who may bite, lick, or chew them should be carefully chosen by the parents.*
   a. Buy toy blocks that are too large to be swallowed. Buy only unpainted blocks.
   b. Buy only unbreakable rattles in order to avoid the availability of beads from a smashed rattle that can be swallowed or aspirated.
   c. Check baby toys for loose nails, beads, or other small parts that can find their way into the baby's mouth and be swallowed.
   d. Avoid strings or cords on crib toys that may loop

around the child's neck and cause choking or strangulation.

e. Avoid pencils, crayons, or similar pointed objects
in the crib.

f. Avoid toys that have small removable parts such as
the glass eyes in stuffed animals.

3. *Other Suggestions:*

a. Frequently inspect toys for loose parts, sharp edges,
or defective wiring. Repair or discard damaged
toys.

b. When not in use, put away all toys and children's
play equipment in a designated area or storage bin.

c. Never leave toys on stairs, floors, or sidewalks where
they can cause accidental injury.

Toys can contribute to every area of child development
and are essential for the physical and mental health of
a child. Parents must make every effort to insure toy
safety for their children. You may obtain information
on hazardous toys by writing to the Toy Safety Review
Committee, Bureau of Product Safety, Food and Drug
Administration, 5401 West Bard Avenue, Bethesda,
Maryland 20016.

9

Accidental Strangulation and Suffocation

Suffocation and choking are the most frequent causes of accidental deaths in children under one year of age. The National Safety Council tells us that hundreds of people die each year from choking on food and that many of these victims are children.

Objects

Suffocation can result when a piece of food lodges in the back of the throat, blocking the victim's airway. Although many of the inhaled objects, such as eggshells, seeds, chicken bones, fish bones, fruit skins, large, improperly chewed pieces of meat, and peanuts, are foods, there is a variety of other foreign bodies listed on page 101 that can be accidentally inhaled by a child.

Choking, strangulation, and suffocation are the result of breathing in a foreign body and can occur in any age bracket from infancy to adult, with the infant bearing the highest risk. The baby who sees a foreign object in his crib will grasp the object and take it to his mouth. The object may then cause him to cough and gag, which can lead to accidental suffocation and a tragic death. The more common culprits found in cribs are diaper pins, straight pins, coins, buttons, seeds, beads, and toys with loosely attached parts.

POTENTIALLY DANGEROUS OBJECTS

Balloons	Coins
Beads	Peanut shells
Beans	Peanuts
Bobby pins	Popcorn
Bones	Screws
Buttons	Straight pins
Carrots	Tacks

Even loose bedclothes in the crib can cause trouble and should be firmly fastened. Anything that can interfere with the child's breathing, such as loose covers or blankets, must be kept away from the baby's face. Do not use a pillow in an infant's crib. The crib mattress should be firm. The infant's carriage should also be kept free of any dangerous objects that can be easily swallowed or interfere with the infant's breathing. Flimsy plastic harnesses, zippered bags, and pillows can smother and suffocate an infant. Never leave diaper pins—opened or closed —near the baby while changing him. Children too young to chew ought never to be given candy containing nuts. Remember that beads, buttons, and coins are not playthings. These precautionary measures, of course, do not preclude giving an infant the benefit of tactile or perceptual stimulation. Safe toys, mobiles, rattles, and dolls that do not easily come apart may be used but should be kept at a distance from the infant.

Feeding

An infant's choking while being fed is not uncommon and can be a real threat to a child's life. An infant in a crib should never be left unattended to feed himself with a propped-up bottle. If the baby, during his feeding, begins to spit up formula and starts coughing or gagging, stop the feeding immediately. Remove the bottle and start again when the child appears comfortable. Mothers should be sure that the nipple openings are not too large; if they are, too much formula will get into the baby's mouth all at once and cause gagging and possible suffocation.

Plastic Bags

Children think that plastic bags, like those dry cleaners use, are fascinating playthings and pull them over their heads. When they do, static electricity is generated that causes the plastic to cling in an adhesive manner to the child's body, resulting in immediate suffocation and death. The more the victim struggles, the more the plastic clings, being too strong for any small child to tear loose.

Fatalities can be prevented if these plastic coverings are destroyed as soon as they come into the house. They should never be used as handy bags or as crib mattress covers. Dr. Paul B. Jeruit, chairman of the Maricopa County (Arizona) Medical Society's Safety Committee, has issued the following warning:

"A child playing with a poisonous snake would not be in as great danger as one playing with a plastic film which clings with such diabolical tenacity. Such needless deaths can be prevented by keeping plastic bags away from children."

Toy Balloons

Toy balloons can also cause suffocation and death. Rubber balloons appear to be ideal playthings for children since they are soft, light, nontoxic, and present no sharp edges. Unfortunately, this is not the case. One nine-month-old infant was found blue and unconscious in his crib by his father. He had been put to bed with a blown-up balloon obtained the same day at the state fair. The father could not find the balloon and realized the child might have been playing with it. Then he noticed bloody mucus coming from the child's nose and mouth and immediately removed a deflated balloon from the back of his throat. After administering mouth-to-mouth resuscitation, the father took the child to a hospital emergency room where all intensive medical efforts failed and the

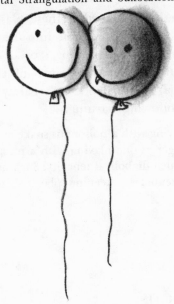

child died fourteen hours later. Another equally tragic case was that of a two-year-old boy found by his father choking and becoming blue with difficulty breathing after he had been playing with a balloon. His father immediately started mouth-to-mouth breathing, then summoned an ambulance that took them to the emergency room of the local hospital. There physicians immediately examined the child and found that there was a small deflated rubber balloon protruding through the windpipe. Fortunately, it had not closed off the airway entirely. The deflated rubber balloon was removed and the boy began to breathe easily again. However, the child had suffered brain damage caused by a lack of oxygen during the time he was unable to breathe properly; he later became blind and suffered convulsive seizures.

Sudden deaths due to foreign bodies lodging in wind-pipes are well recognized and many of these accidents could have been prevented. A child should be taught not to breathe while blowing up a balloon because it can easily be inhaled. The infant or toddler should not be allowed to teethe on or play with an inflated or deflated balloon. Never allow an inflated balloon to be within the confines of a crib or bed in which the child sleeps or plays.

Choking—What to Do

Most deaths caused by choking can be avoided if the problem is recognized immediately. Time is of the essence since the victim's airway is being compromised and he will be dead in a matter of minutes if the airway is completely shut off. If the accident happens at home or in a public place where medical help is not available, an adult should attempt to remove the foreign body from the child's throat. During an episode of choking, quickly pick the child up by the feet, hold his head downward, and slap his back sharply. If the object does not come out, and the coughing and gagging still continues, reach into the child's throat and gently release the impacted substance. There is always the danger of pushing the object farther in, so be careful and go slowly. If it is impossible to remove the object, take the child immediately to the nearest hospital emergency room. In such a situation, common sense, calmness, and immediate intervention go a long way toward saving a child's life.

The Long-Scarf Syndrome

We are often unaware of the risks associated with articles that we use in our daily activities. New vogues,

fads, and fashions frequently produce unsuspected inher-
ent dangers. One example is the fashionable free-flowing
scarf that is usually 6 to 12 feet in length. Physicians call
such a potentially fatal and preventable hazard the "long-
scarf syndrome"—entanglement of a scarf's free-flowing
end into any type of moving machinery such as a car, ski
lift, motorcycle, or snowmobile. Recently, a twelve-year-
old child who was wearing such a scarf was dragged into
the open machinery of a ski lift and strangled. Another
child strangled when her scarf became caught in a car
door. Total airway obstruction and strangulation can
occur when a scarf is caught in the engine of a snowmobile. A teen-ager may sustain severe lacerations and
bruises of the face when his scarf becomes entangled in
the rotating wheel of a stationary motorcycle while he is

inspecting the running machinery. The death rate in eleven cases was an astonishingly high 45 percent. Prevention of the long-scarf syndrome is simple: It consists merely of removing the scarf when near a moving machine.

10

Food Poisoning

Contamination

There is no such illness as "ptomaine" poisoning. The word "ptomaine" pertains to a harmless chemical in decayed food and does not signify a particular type of food poisoning.

Food contamination, on the other hand, is a type of poisoning that can cause serious discomfort to the victim. In addition, food poisoning may also be caused by chemical poisons used in the cultivation of plants, and chemicals from containers in which some foods are stored.

Outbreaks of food poisoning are usually caused by the poisonous substances produced by the staphylococcus strain of bacteria. The foods that provide the best culture media, or breeding places, for these bacteria are ground meat, foods containing various types of salad dressing and cream sauce, cream-filled pastry, cheeses, sausages, rapid-cured hams, and milk. Foods stored without refrigeration for periods of time become contaminated with bacteria. Infected food handlers can also contaminate foods and cause epidemics of food poisoning.

Food contaminants are also found in infant foods. Feeding infants from glass jars containing baby foods that are contaminated or "spoiled" is hazardous. Shoppers who like to smell what the infant is going to eat will unscrew the lid, allowing for contamination of the baby food. Culturing these contaminated foods often reveals a mixture of bacteria including staphylococcus. Do not give an infant food from a jar that looks as if it has been opened or traumatized.

Another real danger involves particles or slivers of glass that may be found in the contents of the jar as a result of chipping about the lid. Damaged glass jars containing baby foods should not be purchased and their contents should certainly not be given to the infant.

The symptoms of food poisoning begin with excessive salivation, nausea, vomiting, retching, prostration, and diarrhea. In the more serious cases of poisoning, the victim may go into shock.

To Prevent Food Poisoning

1. Keep food either very hot or very cold.
2. Don't eat moldy food.
3. Don't refreeze food, particularly pies and stews.
4. Don't purchase dented or swollen cans containing food. This often indicates that the food has gone bad.
5. Don't attempt to tell whether food has been contaminated or not by tasting or smelling it.

6. Store unopened baby foods in a dry, moderately cool place; any leftovers when baby food has been used must be covered and refrigerated immediately.

The Deadly Mushroom

About a hundred fatalities from mushroom poisoning occur annually in the United States. Of the thousands of kinds of mushrooms, only about a dozen are indisputably poisonous. However, to the victims of accidental mushroom poisoning, the dozen that are poisonous can cause misery, discomfort, and sometimes death. The most toxic of all is the tall, graceful *Amanita phalloides,* which grows in patches and singly in the woods and on cultivated land from the spring until fall. It is variable in color, being brightly colored when young and fading as it matures. This species of mushroom contains a toxic substance that is injurious to all body cells, causing abdominal pain, nausea, and vomiting, as well as liver, kidney, and brain damage leading to convulsions and coma.

The story is often told of a family of mushroom collectors, including three teen-aged boys, who often gathered mushrooms near the University of California Los Angeles campus. One night, the family sat down to enjoy their harvest of mushrooms sautéed in butter. The middle son refused even to taste the dish but his parents and two brothers consumed substantial portions. At midnight, the entire family, except the middle son, became violently ill with agonizing intestinal cramps, severe diarrhea, and vomiting. The four victims were rushed to the hospital but despite the efforts of the doctors both adults were dead within a week. The two boys, who had eaten fewer mushrooms, survived. It's a gruesome story, but illustrates that even in the hands of experienced enthusiasts, wild mushrooms can be poisonous.

The amateur mushroom hunter should not believe in old wives' tales when determining whether a mushroom is harmless or not. Some people think that a mushroom is edible if the skin peels easily off the cap. This is not so. Nor is it true that a poisonous mushroom will tarnish a silver spoon or that cooking or drying the plant can remove its poison. A Stanford University physician advised mushroom fanciers on poisoning prevention by stating: "The only place to pick mushrooms is at your grocery store."

Children must never be allowed to pick or eat wild mushrooms since adults are unable to differentiate the edible from the poisonous.

The only sure cure for mushroom poisoning is **never to eat wild mushrooms. There is no specific antidote for mushroom poisoning. The patient should receive emergency supportive treatment at the nearest medical facility.**

Halloween Food Mishaps

Halloween food can cause a great deal of misery to a child who is supposedly making joyous trick-or-treat rounds. It is a fact, though difficult to believe, that children often return from gathering their rewards to find that they have collected poisoned popcorn, booby-trapped apples, or soap-coated candy canes. Every year we read of family tragedies caused by childhood accidents and deaths immediately after Halloween night. One parent in Oneida, New York, expressed shock and dismay when her seven-year-old daughter returned home with an apple containing a concealed sharp pin. Other reports have described popcorn made with mothballs and soap. One Halloween night a ten-year-old lad cut up an apple he had received and found a razor blade inside. A two-and-a-half-year-old toddler wasn't so lucky, however. He suffered mouth cuts after biting into an apple that concealed a razor blade. One newspaper item reported that 400 Ventura, California, parents called police on Halloween to report sabotaged fruit and tack-filled popcorn. These happenings, difficult to accept or understand, are a real threat that can face your child or any child during his trick-or-treat rounds in his own neighborhood.

Suggestions for a Safe Halloween

1. Do not allow children to eat any of the goodies they have collected until they have been carefully examined by an adult.

2. Accompany young children on their rounds. Teach children not to enter any stranger's home and to avoid

the homes of any known cranks or adults who are intolerant of children.

3. Be sure children carry flashlights, and sew glowing tapes on their costumes to increase the children's visibility, thereby helping to prevent accidental injury on roads or streets. Many times youngsters preoccupied with Halloween fun may be careless crossing streets and must be reminded of basic safety rules.

4. Be sure children's costumes are fire-resistant and short enough to prevent tripping. Masks and other facial disguises should not restrict vision or breathing.

11

Animal Hazards

Insect Stings

Insects kill more people in the United States each year than any of the other venom carriers including the rattlesnake. Approximately fifty persons are reported every year to have died following an insect bite, and thousands of other victims suffer severe reactions. Officially, these stinging insects are called hymenoptera, but they are better known and recognized as bees, yellow jackets, wasps, and hornets. These insects are found all over the United States, especially around beach and picnic areas.

The honeybee is a hairy, fuzzy-bodied, golden-brown insect with a blunt abdomen. The wasp is smooth and shiny; it has a sharply tapering abdomen and holds its wings nearly parallel. The color of the yellow jacket explains its name. These insects, particularly the yellow jacket, are attracted to picnickers feasting on hot dogs, hamburgers, or fried chicken. The yellow jacket, especially, is aggressive and dangerous and often annoys those who enjoy outdoor living. Stinging insects are excited by perfumes, hair pomades, quick movements, dark-colored rough clothes, and perspiration.

All insect stings pose a potential danger, and the victim may react in any of the following ways:

1. *The person with a normal reaction* will feel pain and a burning sensation for a short period of time. He will develop a welt about the size of a nickel or dime that will disappear within a few hours.

2. *The person who is sensitive or allergic to insect stings* will experience a severe localized swelling in the area of the bite. This reaction may be connected with abdominal cramps, dizziness, headaches, and a general feeling of weakness or discomfort.

3. *The person who is exquisitely sensitive or allergic* may experience a life-threatening state that involves swelling of the throat, difficulty in breathing, hive reactions, shock, and collapse. Death, if it occurs, comes on suddenly within an hour if emergency measures are not instituted immediately.

Fortunately, in most cases the first allergic reaction following an insect bite may be severe but not fatal and serve as a warning to the victim. *Today, the severely allergic patient can be saved if immediate emergency treatment is available.* Parents must be alert and informed as to how best to manage this life-threatening situation.

Important: If your child or any other member of the family is allergic to insect bites, you should purchase (with a medical prescription) an *insect sting first-aid kit* from your pharmacy. (*See* pages 119, 120.) This kit should always be available to the insect-sensitive individual—whether in his home or when traveling.

If you know that your child is sensitive to the sting of an insect, particularly a bee, yellow jacket, or wasp, consider yourself forewarned. Although most insect bites are

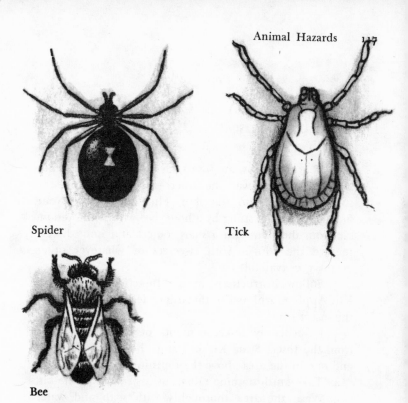

Spider

Tick

Bee

harmless to children, others can be lethal to those who are sensitive to the venom injected. It is important to remember that the wasp's stinger is smooth, resembling a hypodermic needle, and is withdrawn after stinging, but that the honeybee's stinger has a barbed tip that becomes imbedded in the skin, making its withdrawal difficult.

To prevent serious reactions to insect stings, the sensitive individual should seek out immunization treatments. Desensitizing injections have been effective in over 90 percent of the patients receiving this type of therapy. Injections of the insect venom are usually given once weekly in gradually increasing doses until the effective preventive dose is reached. Your physician should be consulted for details.

What to Do When Your Child Is Bitten by an Insect

1. If attacked by an insect, avoid swift movements. If stung, don't swat the insect—this only drives the stinger farther into the skin. Flick it off with your fingers instead. If stung by a honeybee, scrape the venom sac from the skin with a sharp object and immediately remove the stinger with tweezers or whatever other means are available.

2. Follow instructions in the Insect Sting First-Aid Kit: Apply tourniquet to the arm or leg above the site of the insect sting.

3. Immediately inject contents of the two syringes from the Insect Sting Kit, one into the site of the sting and one in the area above the tourniquet.

4. Take antihistamine tablets as instructed in the kit.

5. Wash the area thoroughly with soap and water and apply ice packs to reduce swelling.

6. Limit the patient's movements and quickly seek emergency care in a physician's office or in a hospital emergency room.

CONTENTS OF INSECT STING FIRST-AID KITS

1. A tourniquet.
2. Tweezers.
3. Two disposable syringes and needles with measured amounts of adrenaline.
4. Antihistamine tablets to be taken orally to ward off delayed reactions.
5. Alcohol swab.

After using the kit in an emergency situation, the patient should be taken to the nearest hospital emergency room or physician's office for continued emergency treatment.

Note: People with known insect allergies should always wear an identifying tag. A bracelet indicating the allergy can be obtained from Medic-Alert Foundation, Box 1009, Turlock, California 95380. This type of identification could save a child's life.

HOW TO AVOID INSECT BITES

1. Avoid areas where insects abound, such as beaches, playgrounds, and open fields.
2. Always dress for the occasion, especially for picnicking. Shorts and tank tops are a poor choice; long pants and long-sleeved shirts are far better. Do not wear

Insect Sting First-Aid Kit   (see contents on page 119)

loose-fitting clothes. Wear light instead of dark clothing. Do not go barefoot or wear sandals because bees often forage on clover and other low ground cover.

3. Keep food covered, especially outdoors, and be sure garbage cans are closed and sprayed with insecticides.

4. Avoid substances with strong odors because they attract insects. Do not use perfume, hair spray, hair tonic, or tanning lotion if you are subject to insect bites.

5. Use insect repellents.

6. Drive with the car windows closed.

7. Avoid risky acts, such as tampering with an insect's nest.

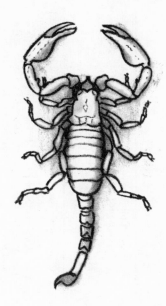

Scorpion

Scorpion Bites

Scorpions can be dangerous and may cause harm, especially to children. These animals normally use their venom for self-defense and for killing their prey. The scorpion will not sting a human being unless provoked. In the United States, there have been few reported cases of scorpion bite. However, in Mexico, there is a species of scorpion that is responsible for severe bite reactions that can be lethal, 94 percent of the reported deaths occurring among children under nine.

After a child is bitten, he often will complain of a tin-

Insect Stings—Symptoms and Treatment

Insect	Description	Symptoms	Treatment
Black Widow Spider	Dark brown to black. Red or yellow hourglass markings on the underside of the female's abdomen. Male does not have this mark and is not poisonous.	Local redness in bite area. Pain. Muscles become rigid. Perspiration and nausea. Difficulty in breathing and talking.	Use antiseptic on the bitten area. Keep victim quiet and call a doctor.
Scorpion	Crablike appearance with claw-like pincers. Solid yellow or yellow with irregular stripes on back.	A dangerously toxic sting may not change the appearance of the area. Excessive salivation, facial contortions, nervous exhaustion.	Keep victim quiet and call doctor immediately. Antitoxin given by physicians is effective in treatment.
Bee	Winged body with yellow and black stripes. Covered with feathery hairs.	Burning and itching with swelling in the bite area. Usually leaves venom sac in victim. Nausea, vomiting, hives, difficulty in breathing, and shock.	Gently scrape the stinger so the venom sac can be removed without being squeezed. Wash area with antiseptic. Contact doctor immediately. Keep victim warm and calm. Emergency care essential.
Tick	Oval with small head. Gray or brown body.	Attaches itself to the skin and sucks blood. After removal there is danger of infection if mouth parts are left in the wound.	Apply heated needle to tick. Gently remove with tweezers. Wash area with soap and water, apply antiseptic.

gling and burning sensation extending up the arm or leg. Within hours, the patient experiences generalized spasms, pain, nausea, vomiting, and convulsions. These symptoms may last for one to ten days.

Although frightening, scorpion stings are not serious if treated immediately. If a bite is visible after contact with a scorpion and you suspect venom has been injected, apply strong ammonia and cold compresses to the bite, keep the child as quiet as possible, and take him immediately to a hospital or physician for treatment.

Dog Bites

Almost half a million people in the United States are bitten by family or stray dogs every year. For the most part the victims are children who petted a dog while he was eating, startled him when asleep, teased him, or in some other way mistreated the animal. When he is provoked, hurt, frightened, or confused, a pet's natural instincts may cause him to snap. One must also be wary of injured pets. The gentlest of pets maddened by fear and pain can bite a child.

Dog bites are not only frightening and painful but may also be dangerous. Although the incidence of rabies in the United States is quite small, the risk of developing rabies after a dog bite is a real one. Rabies is a serious medical problem and it necessitates treatment with anti-rabies vaccine that is lifesaving. Therefore, if a child is bitten by a dog, the police and health departments should be notified immediately. In cases where the dog is available, testing is essential to determine whether he has rabies. If the dog cannot be found, the physician has to decide whether the victim should be given a series of antirabies-vaccine injections.

Pets must be chosen to suit the environment and the family unit. The choice of a dog should take into consideration the breed of the animal, his natural temperament, and his tolerance for children. Dog owners should assume responsibility for preventing accidental injury to a child by training the dog, keeping the pet on a leash, and securing the necessary vaccinations against rabies for the dog.

RULES FOR PREVENTION OF DOG BITES

1. Teach children not to abuse or tease dogs. They should be taught how to handle and be gentle to their pets.
2. Don't attempt to pull a ball, a stick, or other objects out of the dog's mouth.
3. Don't take food away from a dog or bother him while he is eating.
4. Don't interfere in a dog fight.
5. Don't wake a dog up suddenly.

What to Do for a Dog Bite

1. Wash the wound at once with soap and water. Apply pressure dressings for any excessive bleeding.

2. Go immediately to a physician or hospital emergency room for further treatment.

3. Be able to identify the dog and his owner. Report particulars of the incident to the local police and health authorities.

12

Safety in the Home

The Nursery

A newborn infant is totally dependent on his parents or guardians for his proper growth, protection, and development. With growth and development comes increased potential for accidents, particularly during the crucial period when the baby's curiosity blossoms and he begins to grasp, reach, and crawl. It is important for a mother to understand the infant's inborn need to explore, and not to underestimate her child.

One infant was recently admitted to a hospital emergency room because he was able to reach through the bars of his crib and grab an electric cord, which he put into his mouth and began biting. The infant bit through the cord and suffered serious electrical burns and shock. As a result, his mouth was permanently scarred to half its normal size.

Infants will reach out and grasp any objects that are in sight. Heavy appliances, such as vaporizers, electric heaters, bottle warmers, irons, toasters, or coffeepots have

CURIOSITY

no place being near any infant. Severe burns can result from the child's pulling and playing with any of these electrical appliances.

Other innocent-looking household items, such as tablecloths and venetian blinds, may cause accidents if the infant is able to reach and play with them. A baby's tugging and pulling on a tablecloth can cause hot liquids to spill, heavy objects to fall, and serious injury to the infant. Toddlers can easily hang themselves with the alluring and easily accessible cords of venetian blinds. Venetian blinds should be kept out of the nursery, as should strings of any type, particularly when they are within reach of the crib or playpen.

Dislocated or fractured legs and arms have frequently been caused by the infant's determined efforts to reach out of a crib or playpen to grasp a particular object. Children have also been accidentally strangled when their heads and necks have been caught between the slats of a crib or playpen. According to the 1973 report of the President's National Commission on Product Safety, the slats of a child's crib or playpen should be a maximum of three inches apart. The cautious mother must be aware of potential hazard and be sure that there are no slats in the infant's crib wide enough to endanger the child's movements. Crib bumpers are also very helpful in preventing accidental injury to the infant.

Bathing a Child in Safety

1. Never bathe an infant for the first time without supervision. It may be a trying experience for both mother and baby, and possibly a dangerous one. An additional precautionary measure is always to hold the infant with one hand while sponging him with the other.

2. To avoid burning the infant, always test the temperature of the water with your elbow before exposing him to it. The water should be at body temperature.

3. When bathing an older child in the bathtub, always place a bath mat or folded bath towel on the bottom of the tub to prevent slipping.

4. Never leave a child unattended in the bathtub, even for a second. Ignore the telephone or doorbell when you are bathing your child.

Safeguarding the Infant— Safety Begins in the Cradle

1. The infant must never be left alone—especially during periods of diaper change, feeding, and weighing. Never leave the baby unattended for any reason. If left

alone, even for a moment, the infant can roll off onto the floor and in that moment disaster can strike.

2. Do not use flimsy or constricting bedclothes, or harnesses or pillows, in the crib.

3. Keep dangerous objects such as heavy appliances, plastic bags, or cords out of reach of a child, whether an infant or a toddler.

4. Do not use paint containing lead for nursery walls. Prevent lead poisoning.

5. Be sure crib and playpen slats are close enough together to prevent the child from sticking his head or limbs through and getting trapped between them. Too much space between slats can be a death trap. Keep the crib sides up at all times. Use a protective playpen as often as possible—it is a most ingenious, safe, and practical piece of baby furniture.

6. Feed an infant slowly, while holding him in the crook of the arm. Never prop a bottle, leaving an infant to feed himself in the crib.

7. If the nursery is not within hearing distance of the parents' bedroom, install an intercom system. Parents must be able to hear the cries of a distressed infant during the night, or be aware of an overly quiet infant during the day.

Falls

Falls are the second leading cause of accidental deaths, killing more children than any other kind of accident except traffic accidents. Falls from open windows, particularly, have resulted in more injury and death to our children than many of the infectious diseases. Such deaths in the toddler age group far exceed the toll from the more publicized accidents due to fire, poisoning, or drowning. Children do not bounce; they are not pliable; when they fall from open windows they may suffer skull fractures, possibly brain damage, dislocation or fractures of the extremities, as well as internal injuries. Homes with windows carelessly left open are likely places for tragic accidents. This problem is not limited to children who live in apartments. It can happen anywhere, particularly during the summer months when toddlers are attracted to the open window.

The following accident reports are not uncommon when one studies the log of the emergency room of any hospital. An eighteen-month-old boy was sitting on the back of a sofa, leaning backward against a screen in an open window. The screen ripped and he fell three stories onto the dirt alongside the house. Fortunately he survived. A three-year-old girl climbed on a radiator and leaned against a screen, which gave away. She fell three stories and died. When a sixteen-month-old boy was able to loosen a screen in a kitchen window, he fell two stories to the sidewalk below and died of a skull fracture. Others were luckier—such as the eighteen-month-old child who was hanging on the inside of a windowsill of a second-floor apartment and suddenly went through a screen, tumbling to the ground. Luckily, the baby landed in soft dirt and survived.

There are other, almost miraculous, stories of children who have survived long falls—especially if they were fortunate enough to fall on soft ground instead of a hard surface. In all these cases the one common denominator,

the one definitive causative agent—particularly concerning young children—is that they were all unattended when they fell.

HOW TO PREVENT A CHILD
FROM FALLING OUT OF A WINDOW
IN YOUR HOME

1. Make sure that all screens are secure and in good repair. However, don't rely on them to prevent any child from falling.

2. Never place a child's bed or crib next to a window.

3. Avoid placing any type of furniture near windows. If you must have open windows where a small child is either sleeping or playing, open them from the top. If opened from the bottom, be sure they are not up more than five inches, and that there are safety gadgets to keep the child from raising them any further.

4. Provide some sort of metal protective screen or fencing, particularly if windows must be open during the summer months, or if they are close to the floor.

5. Keep an eye on any child who is near or on his way to an open window.

Children are injured in falls other than from a window. They trip over objects left on the floor, they slip on highly waxed floors or on spilled grease, they fall off unstable or improperly placed ladders. Children also fall from banisters, out of trees, from the tops of fences. A toddler is always falling down and usually possesses a multiplicity of bumps and bruises.

HOW TO PREVENT A CHILD FROM FALLING

1. Avoid highly waxed floors or stairways. Immediately wipe up all liquids spilled on the floor. Stray toys should be picked up and the child should be taught to place them in a safe area. Anchor small throw rugs. Repair worn carpets and install mats at all doorways to cut down on the amount of slippery surfaces that the child may encounter.

2. Your stairwells should have handrails; they should be on both sides if the stairs are wide. Inside stairs

should be well lighted with a switch at the top and bottom. Repair broken stairways, loose floorboards, and wobbly railings. Stairs should always be kept clear of tripping hazards and they should be carpeted.

3. Do not allow children to climb ladders—they are not playthings. In any case, ladders should be kept in good condition and properly placed when in use.

4. Keep children away from places where they are likely to fall; don't allow crawlers on stairs; keep children off banisters, out of trees, off the tops of fences, away from windowsills.

5. Set gates at the top and bottom of stairs until children can climb safely. Make sure window screens are secure. Use sturdy guard railings at low windows.

Fires and Burns

CHILDREN ARE NOT FIREPROOF

Fires and accidental burns can happen anytime and anywhere. Private homes catch on fire every fifty-seven seconds in the United States and the unfortunate victims are usually children. In one year an estimated 6,000 deaths from fires and burns occurred in American homes. These fires happen so often that one can easily say that children are continuously being threatened by the multiple causes of fires in the home. Such fires most frequently are caused by faulty heaters and cooking equipment, careless smoking habits, misuse of electrical appliances, children playing with matches, careless storage of rubbish including flammable liquids, and faulty roofs and chimneys.

The kitchen is a particularly dangerous area for painful burns to occur. The source of injury is usually scalding hot water, hot foods, hot grease, or direct flash burns from a stove. Small children pull pots full of hot food down upon themselves by grabbing visible pot handles. When hot cooking pots and pans are on the stove, turn their handles around so they face the rear of the stove. Then they are out of the line of traffic and away from children's reaching hands or an inadvertent bump.

Most often the scaldings that happen outside the kitchen area but within the home result when a child turns on a hot-water tap. Recently, a mother put her two-year-old child in the bathtub for her routine bath. The tub contained about six inches of lukewarm water. The mother left the room for a few minutes to get a glass to rinse the baby's hair and when she returned she found the hot water running and the little girl lying on her back in the tub. The child died eight hours later at the hospital with severe burns over 80 percent of her body. Thousands of children are burned accidentally by bathwater every year because parents are unaware of the possible dangers of leaving a child alone in the bathtub. Parents must accept the fact that hot water is a serious hazard in any home and take precautions to avoid a potential burn accident.

Remember: If you live in a house, don't allow your water heater to exceed 140° F. When bathing your child, run the cool water first and then let the hot water run until it is warm enough to bathe in. The valve that controls the running water should allow the hot and cold

mixture of water to come out of one faucet. Never leave a child alone in the bathtub for any reason.

Children who play with matches and the careless smoker account for one out of every five home fires. Children often set fires playing with matches, cigarette lighters, and pilot lights, especially when there is no adult around. Matches and lighters should be kept out of reach and out of sight of children.

Rubbish fires are responsible for the destruction of many homes. The piles of old newspapers, magazines, discarded furniture, toys, and clothing that are usually stored around the house are firetraps. Highly flammable liquids such as oils, paints, paint thinners, and cleaning fluids of all kinds should be stored in capped metal cans in an area that is "off limits" to children and smokers.

Potentially flammable materials should never be stored under stairways, in hallways, or in closets.

Grease fires are particularly dangerous because they are difficult to control and cause severe burn injuries.

What to Do in Case of a Grease Fire

1. Turn off the stove or oven. Cover the burning pan or close the flaming oven, taking care not to get yourself burned. Never carry a burning pan to the sink or outdoors.

2. Throw baking soda on the blaze. Packages of baking soda should be kept handy for such an unexpected emergency.

3. Use a dry chemical fire extinguisher. Fire extinguishers should be in every kitchen and should be easily accessible. Older children should be taught to use them.

4. Remember that fires caused by liquids such as greases, oils, gasoline, and paints have to be smothered with baking soda or a dry chemical fire extinguisher. **Never douse with water, which will spread the fire.**

What to Do If a Child's Clothes Catch on Fire

1. Don't allow the child to run or make any movements, since these motions will fan the fire and intensify the flames.

2. Quickly have the child fall to the floor and roll over and over with arms folded on the chest and face protected.

3. Smother the flames by wrapping the victim in a rug, coat, or heavy blanket.

In case of fire there are three basic steps to take:

Step 1. Put out the blaze as quickly as you can, using the correct method for the particular type of fire.

Step 2. Make sure the children and others get out of the house and somebody calls the fire department immediately.

Step 3. If fire spreads, rescue all present in the home and escape through nearest safe exit. Remain calm, walk quickly, don't run.

ESCAPE

If people were taught how to escape from burning homes, most home fire injuries and burns could be prevented. To get everyone out of the house safely in case of a fire, you must have a family escape plan with instructions to each child on how to leave the house. It may save the life of one of your children. The family escape plan must include five basic points: (1) a floor plan of the house indicating all floors, windows, porches, stairways, and fire escapes; (2) alternate escape routes; (3) fire practice drills; (4) special care procedures for the very young and the elderly; and (5) an agreed-upon meeting place outside the house where all must assemble.

Ways of reaching the ground from every room must be clearly detailed. A chain fire ladder that can be hooked over any window sill may be a safe means of escape in time of emergency. The ladder can be stored in a small box under the window or in a closet. If windows cannot be opened for whatever reason, advise the members of your family to use a shoe, chair, or other object to break the glass and clear off the jagged edges. Make sure children are instructed in opening doors, windows, or screens as escape routes.

First Aid for Burns

First degree burns should be treated by immersing the burned area immediately in cold water. Cold compresses can then be applied to the area. After the pain subsides, the burn can be blotted dry and covered with sterile dressings.

Second degree burns require medical care. Blisters usually develop over the burn area, which may involve 10 percent or more of the child's body. Contamination and infection are the usual complications necessitating the need of immediate medical care. Blisters must not be broken. The burn should be covered with sterile dressings.

Third degree burns cause deep tissue damage of a very serious nature. The victim must be given immediate medical care. Dry sterile dressings to exclude possible air contamination should be applied while seeking help in a doctor's office or in the emergency room of a local hospital. Do not apply cold compresses.

BASIC CHECKLIST FOR FIRE PREVENTION IN THE HOME

1. Keep combustible material outside the home, enlisting children's help to keep basements and attics orderly

and free of debris. Keep stove area free of grease and flammable substances.

2. Store matches and lighters out of reach of small children. Don't let children play with stoves.

3. Never leave small children alone even for a moment.

4. Keep bedroom doors closed at night. Check bedroom doors frequently to see that they close and open properly.

5. Don't allow smoking or lighting of matches in attics, closets, or other confined places where flammable material may be stored.

6. Don't allow anyone to smoke in bed. Have large deep ash trays available for discarded cigarette stubs. Wastebaskets should never be used for smoldering butts.

7. Keep fire extinguishers in places where they are

easily accessible, with instructions on how to use them in case of an emergency.

8. Post fire instructions and emergency telephone numbers in clear view of children, preferably adjacent to the phone.

Electrical Accidents

Electrical wiring causes 13 percent of all fires. Fires can start quickly if you misuse electricity. An extension cord that is disconnected from the appliance but plugged into the wall can cause grave electrical burns and shock to young, unsuspecting children. Worn or exposed wires on electrical appliances or on extension cords can cause an electrical accident. Electrical appliances that are used near or fall into water can cause severe shock.

HOW TO PREVENT
ELECTRICAL ACCIDENTS

1. Never use a radio, TV, heater or any other electrical appliance near a tub, sink, or pool. Keep hands dry when operating electrical tools, switches, or appliances. Remember water and electricity don't mix.

2. Electric cords should be checked periodically and any worn or exposed wires should be repaired. Handle electrical wires as though they were powerful and in need of continuous care.

3. Unused electric wall outlets should be capped or sealed with electric tape to prevent children from inserting metal objects into them.

4. Never use a knife or fork to pry toast from a plugged-in toaster.

5. Never leave an extension cord plugged into wall when disconnected from the appliance. Always unplug the cord at the wall outlet after using the appliance.

6. Major appliances should be installed and repaired by professional servicemen.

7. Do not overload your electrical appliance. Fuses blow because they are the safety valves of your electrical circuits. If fuses continue to blow, have a qualified electrician locate the trouble.

Drownings

There has been an increasing incidence of accidental drownings primarily due to an extensive growth in the number of pool users, especially children. Approximately 700 people drown in swimming pools each year, most of them in private residential pools. Unfortunately, children under five are the usual victims. One half of all these pool drownings could have been prevented.

The more common causes of pool drownings are: lack of qualified adult supervision; absence of adequate safeguards such as fences and rescue equipment; and the inability of the victim to swim or float.

Stories of children drowning often include the sad information that they were alone when found, that there were no self-latching gates at the pool, or that an adult forgot to lock the gate of the fence surrounding the pool area. The single most frequent cause of accidental drownings is leaving the child unattended, even for a few seconds.

The number of deaths can certainly be reduced if a concerted effort is made by pool owners, parents, and children to be aware of and accept safety practices.

HOW TO PREVENT ACCIDENTAL DROWNINGS IN A POOL

1. Put up a fence that is at least 6 feet high and built with vertical or solid segments. Fences with fancy basket weaves, split railings, or chain links, which children can easily climb, should be avoided. To be a safety measure, a fence must be properly designed to keep small children out and make it difficult for older children to trespass.

2. The fence must have self-closing and self-latching gates with the mechanism out of reach of children. The gate should be securely locked when the pool is not in use.

3. A pool cover can serve as protection for a child who trespasses when the pool is not being used.

4. The shallow and deep ends of the pool should be clearly marked to show safe jumping and diving areas. Diving into pools and striking the pool bottom or its walls has caused serious head injuries, paralysis, and death.

5. The pool bottom should slope gradually. A float line is essential to keep younger swimmers in the shallow end.

6. There should be clear and strict instructions prohibiting any horseplay around the slippery pool area.

7. Children should be taught swimming, floating, and water survival techniques at an early age.

8. Rescue equipment to use in case of an accidental drowning should be prominently displayed poolside.

Emergency numbers of local rescue squads, ambulances, and physicians should be posted on a nearby telephone.

9. Clean and repair your pool regularly. Slippery bottoms, faulty float lines, and burned-out underwater lamps account for a number of pool accidents.

10. An alarm system in the pool which will sound an alert in case someone falls into the pool by accident can be an excellent safety precaution.

What to Do in Case of an Accidental Drowning

1. Quickly throw rescue equipment to a floundering swimmer. Call for help. Have someone phone the rescue emergency squad or ambulance.

2. After rescue, remain calm. Keep the victim warm and administer artificial respiration if he is having trouble breathing.

Artificial respiration means breathing with the help of another person. It can be life-saving to the victim in respiratory distress. Mouth-to-mouth rescue breathing is necessary in many cases of accidental drowning.

How to Give Mouth-to-Mouth Resuscitation

1. Place the victim on his back with his head tilted back—a folded coat or blanket under the victim's shoulders will tilt the head back in the proper position for mouth-to-mouth resuscitation.

2. The mouth should be cleared and the tongue pulled forward.

3. Begin mouth-to-mouth resuscitation by breathing into the victim's mouth until the victim begins to breathe by himself. Continue at three-to-five second intervals.

Firearm Accidents in the Home

Most firearm accidents don't occur on the target range or in the hunting field but right in the home. The 1971 edition of *Accident Facts,* which is published annually by the National Safety Council, indicates that there were 2,300 firearm fatalities in the preceding year. Out of this total, 1,200 occurred in the home and 900 in the field. Firearms are the fifth ranking cause of death in the home.

Thousands of air rifles are given to youngsters each year in the belief that an air rifle is not a gun. The casual attitude toward these guns is responsible for many injuries. Air-rifle pellets—bee-bees—may not penetrate a target but ricochet unpredictably and cause serious eye injuries. Target shooting is fun, but it can be a safe pas-time only if parents see to it that all guns, including air rifles, are used properly and under supervision.

THE DO'S AND DON'TS OF FIREARM SAFETY IN THE HOME

1. Make certain that guns in the house are unloaded. All guns should be unloaded before being brought into the home.

2. Always store guns out of reach of children. Lock them up.

3. Be aware of the gun's accident potential. Teach your children to treat every gun as if it were loaded.

4. Always keep the gun pointed in a safe direction.

5. Protect the family by teaching them how to handle firearms safely.

What to Do in Case of a Gunshot Wound

1. Cover the wound immediately with a sterile pressure bandage.

2. Control any bleeding by applying a tourniquet above the wound.

3. Do not move the victim—keep him warm and try to prevent any panic and fear.

4. Call a doctor immediately, or transfer the victim to the nearest hospital emergency room.

5. Don't try to remove the bullet and don't try to administer any type of first aid to the open wound.

13

Teaching the Child to Deal with an Emergency

It is most important that children be taught to handle certain types of emergencies, particularly when the parents are not available. The average four-year-old child is capable of understanding much more than his parents probably believe. A five-year-old youngster should be able to state his name and address, and should be taught to dial "O" for the telephone operator in case of emergency. When you teach your child to handle emergencies, your approach must be calm and matter-of-fact. The child should develop an attitude of awareness rather than one of anxiety or fear.

A child should be taught to recognize potential dangers and what must be done by him to cope with unexpected emergencies. For example:

If he is lost in the country, he should remain in the open where he can be found more easily.

If he is bitten by an animal, he should not hide the injury from his parents but should report it to an adult as soon as possible and try to identify the biting animal.

A child should never become friendly with strangers. He should not accept automobile rides, candy, money, or favors.

In case of a fire at home, a child should know escape routes from the bedroom. He should be told how to dial for the fire department and how to report the exact location of the house. If his clothes catch on fire, he should be taught to fall to the ground and smother the flames by rolling about. If a rug or coat is handy, he should wrap these around his body.

Keeping emergency telephone numbers visible at all times and taking a few minutes to speak to your child concerning what he should do in an emergency can go a long way in preventing family tragedies.

Appendix
Poison Control Centers

(Government Printing Office, Washington, D.C.)

City	Name and Address	Telephone	Director and Assistant Director
	ALABAMA		
STATE COORDINATOR	State Department of Public Health Montgomery 36104	265–2341	Miss Jo Strickland, Division of Accident Prevention
Anniston	Poison Control Center Anniston Memorial Hospital Pharmacy Department 400 E. 10th St. P.O. Box 370 36201	237–5421 Ext. 382	Bill Stephenson, R. Ph. Wendell Turner, R. Ph.
Auburn	Poison Control Center School of Pharmacy Auburn University 36830	826–4740	Byron B. Williams, Jr., Ph.D. Joseph E. Manno, Ph.D.
Birmingham	Poison Control Center Children's Hospital 1601 6th Ave., S. 35233	323–8901	S. D. Palmer, M.D. P. A. Palmisano, M.D.
Dothan	Poison Control Center Southeast Alabama General Hospital 36301	794–3131 Ext. 521	Dean H. Byrd, Sr. Dorothy West, R.N.

Florence ....Poison Control Center   764–8321   Jesse H. Thornton, R. Ph.
                     Eliza Coffee Memorial Hospital Ext. 206
                     600 W. Alabama St. 35630

Gadsden ....Poison Control Center   492–1240   J. Barry Jacobs, R. Ph.
                    Baptist Memorial Hospital   Ext. 206   J. Richard Anderson, R. Ph.
                    1007 Goodyear Ave. 35903

Mobile ....Poison Control Center   473–0341   Mrs. Barakeh
                    Mobile General Hospital   Ext. 243
                    St. Anthony & Broad Sts. 36603

ALASKA

STATE
COORDINATOR ...State Department of Health and   586–6311   Thomas McCabe, M.D.
                    Welfare   Chief, Section of Child Health
                    Juneau 99801

Anchorage ....Poison Control Center   279–6661   Gloria K. Park, M.D.
                    Alaska Native Medical Center   Ext. 208,   Allan R. Frost, M.D.
                    Public Health Service   209, 210,
                    Box 7–741 95501   211

Fairbanks ....Poison Control Center   456–6655   Stella Muckenthaler, R.N.
                    Fairbanks Community Hospital   Ext. 35
                    119 North Cushman 99701

Juneau ....Poison Control Center   586–2611   Kenneth Moss, M.D.
                    Greater Juneau Borough Hospital   Mrs. Jennie Smith, R.N.
                    419 6th St. 99801

City	Name and Address	Telephone	Director and Assistant Director
(Alaska—Continued)			
Ketchikan	Poison Information Center Ketchikan General Hospital 3100 Tongass Ave. 99901	225-5171 Ext. 31	Mrs. Clara Diaz, R.N. Mrs. Jean Standerfer, R.N.
Mt. Edgecumbe	Poison Control Center Alaska Native Hospital Public Health Service 99835	966-8347	Roger L. Dinwiddie, R. Ph. Douglass J. Stennett, R. Ph.

ARIZONA

City	Name and Address	Telephone	Director and Assistant Director
STATE COORDINATOR	University of Arizona Tucson 85721	884-0111	Albert L. Picchioni, Ph.D. Professor of Pharmacology
Douglas	Poison Control Center Douglas Hospital 610 9th St. 85607	364-2421	Carl W. Ahl, M.D. Tommy Espinosa, R. Ph.
Flagstaff	Poison Control Center Flagstaff Hospital 1215 N. Beaver St. 86001	744-5233	George H. Yard, M.D. Don Piper, R. Ph.

Ganado	Poison Control Center Project Hope Sage Memorial Hospital Box 457 86505	755-3411	Louis Allen, M.D. Thomas Baynham, R. Ph.
Kingman	Poison Control Center Mohave General Hospital 301 W. Beale 86441	753-6132 Ext. 245 265	Arthur Ellico, R. Ph. Arlene Mornick, R. Ph. Linda Long, R.N.
Nogales	Poison Control Center St. Joseph's Hospital Target Range Rd. P.O. Box 1809 85621	287-2771 Ext. 94	Mrs. Brenda Coulter, R.N. Mrs. Josephine Brubaker, R.N.
Phoenix	Poison Control Center Good Samaritan Hospital 1033 E. McDowell Rd. 85006	252-6611 Ext. 221	Charles Barry, R. Ph. Donald Schaller, M.D.
	Poison Control Center Maricopa County General Hospital 3435 W. Durango 85009	272-6611 Ext. 317	Leonard E. Rothwell, R. Ph. Doris Parker, R.N.
	Poison Control Center Memorial Hospital 1200 S. 5th Ave. 85003	252-5911	Albert C. Asendorf, M.D.
	Poison Control Center St. Joseph's Hospital 350 W. Thomas Rd. 85013	277-6611 Ext. 581	J. B. Waldmann, M.D. Peter Uyehara, R. Ph.

City	Name and Address	Telephone	Director and Assistant Director
(Arizona—Continued)			
Phoenix	Poison Control Center St. Luke's Hospital Medical Center 525 N. 18th St. 85006	258-7373 Ext. 291	W. James Bursey, M.D.
Prescott	Poison Control Center Yavapai Community Hospital 1003 Willow Creek Rd. 86301	445-2700 Ext. 25 58	Edward Ritter, M.D. Donald Morgan, R. Ph.
Tucson	Poison Control Center Pima County General Hospital 2900 S. 6th Ave. 85713	624-2721 Ext. 220	Mario P. Valdez, M.D. E. Kraus, R. Ph.
	Poison Information Center College of Pharmacy University of Arizona 85721	884-0111 Ext. 1427	Albert L. Picchioni, Ph.D. Lincoln Chin, Ph.D.
	Poison Control Center St. Mary's Hospital 1700 W. St. Mary's Rd. 85703	622-5833 Ext. 724	Geri Marconi, R. Ph. Lillian Kennedy, R.N.
	Poison Control Center Tucson Medical Center E. Grant Rd. at Beverly Blvd. 85716	327-5461 Ext. 428	Charles Pullen, M.D. Mrs. Bernice Walworth, R.N.

Winslow ....Poison Control Center   289-2821   Jane Soehner, R.N.
                    Winslow Memorial Hospital   Mabyn Peart, R.N.
                    116 E. Hillview St. 86047

Yuma   ....Poison Control Center   782-1811   Dale Webb, M.D.
                    Parkview Hospital   Ext. 259   Fred Trounstine, R. Ph.
                    Avenue A & 24th St. 85364

ARKANSAS

STATE
COORDINATOR ...State Board of Health   661-2242   James E. Stewart, Jr.
                    Little Rock 72201   Health Educator

El Dorado ....Poison Control Center   863-3161   A. R. Clowney, M.D.
                    Warner Brown Hospital   Ext. 210   Sister M. Joleen, R.N.
                    460 West Oak St. 71730

Fort Smith ....Poison Control Center   782-3071   James M. Post, M.D.
                    St. Edward's Mercy Hospital   Ext. 214,
                    1411 Rogers Ave. 72901   215

                    Poison Control Center   782-2088   James M. Post, M.D.
                    Sparks Regional Medical Center   Ext. 381   Mathew M. Griffin, II, R. Ph.
                    1311 S. Eye St. 72901

Harrison ....Poison Control Center   365-6141   Joe B. Wilson, M.D.
                    Boone County Hospital   Ext. 120
                    620 N. Willow St. 72601

City	Name and Address	Telephone	Director and Assistant Director
(Arkansas—Continued)			
Helena	Poison Control Center Helena Hospital Hospital Dr. 72342	338-6411 Ext. 271	L. J. Pat Bell, M.D. Betty Schaffhauser, R.N.
Little Rock	Poison Control Center Dept. of Pediatrics University of Arkansas Medical Center 4301 W. Markham St. 72205	664-5000 Ext. 415	J. O. Cooper, M.D.
Osceola	Poison Control Center Osceola Memorial Hospital 611 Lee Ave., W. 72370	563-2611 Ext. 53	Lorenzo D. Massey, M.D. Rosalie Tucker
Pine Bluff	Poison Control Center Jefferson Hospital 1515 W. 42nd Ave. 71601	535-6800 Ext. 223, 224, 225	T. F. Townsend, M.D.

CALIFORNIA

City	Name and Address	Telephone	Director and Assistant Director
STATE COORDINATOR ...	Department of Public Health Berkeley 94704	843-7900	Lee E. Farr, M.D., Chief Emergency Health Services Unit

Fresno .... Poison Control Center 233-0911   J. J. Bocian, M.D.
                  Fresno Community Hospital Ext. 2374
                  Fresno & R Sts. Night:
                  P.O. Box 1232 93715 233-7547   R. F. Burns, M.D.
                                       439-3527   Paul K. Greening, M.D.
                                       439-3539

Los Angeles ...... Poison Control Center 664-2121   William Bucher, M.D.
                   Thos. J. Fleming Memorial Center Mrs. Corrine Ray, R.N.
                   Childrens Hospital of Los Angeles
                   P.O. Box 54700
                   4650 Sunset Blvd. 90054

Oakland .... Poison Control Center 652-8171   David Singman, M.D.
                  Alameda–Contra Costa Medical Peter Rosendale
                  Assn.
                  6230 Claremont Ave. 94618

                  Poison Control Center 654-5600   Robert H. Gersden, M.D.
                  Children's Hospital of East Bay Ext. 343
                  51st & Grove Sts. 94609

Orange .... Poison Control Center 633-9393   Herman W. Rannels, M.D.
                 Orange County Medical Center Ext. 273   W. T. Hill, Jr.
                 101 S. Manchester Ave. 92668

San Francisco ...... Poison Control Center 431-2800   Earl Blake, R.N.
                     Central Emergency Hospital
                     135 Polk St. 94102

City	Name and Address	Telephone	Director and Assistant Director
(California—Continued)			
San Francisco	Poison Control Center Children's Hospital 3700 California St. 94119	387–8700	John C. Bolton, M.D.
San Jose	Poison Control Center Santa Clara Valley Medical Center 751 S. Bascom Ave. 95128	293–0262 Ext. 318 or 319	Robert S. Sharkey, M.D. Mrs. Lenore Schiro, R.N.

CANAL ZONE

City	Name and Address	Telephone	Director and Assistant Director
Balboa Heights	Poison Information Center Gorgas Hospital Box 0	2–2600	Daniel Hirschl, M.D.

COLORADO

City	Name and Address	Telephone	Director and Assistant Director
STATE COORDINATOR	State Department of Public Health Denver 80220	388–6111	Valentin E. Wohlauer, M.D. Chief, Emergency Health Services Section and Injury Control Program

Alamosa	Poison Control Center Alamosa Community Hospital 1st & Creston Sts. 81101	589–2511 Ext. 54	R. B. Bradshaw, M.D. Mary Ann Lee, R.N.
Aurora	Poison Control Center L. K. Professional Pharmacy 9240 E. Colfax Ave. 80010	366–1531	Kenneth C. Suher, R. Ph. R. L. McConnell, R. Ph.
Cortez	Poison Control Center Southwest Memorial Hospital 925 S. Broadway 81321	565–3448	V. E. Gardner, M.D. Walter E. Linderholm, R. Ph.
Denver	Poison Control Center Department of Health & Hospitals 6th & Cherokee Sts. 80204	893–6000	John R. Connell, M.D. Harry J. Umlauf, M.D.
	Poison Control Center St. Anthony's Hospital 4231 W. 16th Ave. 80204	825–9011 Ext. 2387	Daniel Dracon, M.D. J. J. Goetzinger
	Poison Control Center University of Colorado Medical Center 4200 E. 9th Ave. 80220	399–1211	Daniel T. Teitelbaum, M.D.
Grand Junction	Poison Control Center St. Mary's Hospital 7th & Patterson Rd. 81501	242–1197 Ext. 715	Donald F. Mayer, R. Ph.
Greeley	Poison Control Center Weld County General Hospital 16th St. at 17th Ave. 80631	352–4121 Ext. 648	Edgar M. Cleaver, M.D. Donald E. Cook, M.D.

City	Name and Address	Telephone	Director and Assistant Director
(Colorado—Continued)			
Longmont	Poison Control Center Longmont Community Hospital 1950 W. Mt. View Ave. 80501	776-1422 Ext. 46	Loy E. Moore, R. Ph.
Pueblo	Poison Control Center 129 Colorado Ave. 81005	542-8680 Ext. 729	Samuel Nelson, M.D.

CONNECTICUT

City	Name and Address	Telephone	Director and Assistant Director
STATE COORDINATOR ...	State Department of Health Hartford 06115	566-3456	Arthur S. Blank Technical Director
Bridgeport	Poison Control Center Bridgeport Hospital 267 Grant St. 06602	334-0131	Francis P. A. Williams, M.D. Sally A. Tarick, R.N.
	Poison Control Center St. Vincent's Hospital 2820 Main St. 06606	336-1081	Leonard F. Del Vecchio, M.D.
Danbury	Poison Control Center Danbury Hospital 95 Locust Ave. 06810	744-2300	Fred C. Spannaus, M.D.

Hartford	Poison Control Center St. Francis Hospital 114 Woodland St. 06105	249-8281	James E. O'Brien, M.D., Ph.D.
	Poison Information Center State Department of Health State Office Bldg. 06115	566-3456	Estelle Siker, M.D. Arthur S. Blank
Middletown	Poison Control Center Middlesex Memorial Hospital 28 Crescent St. 06457	347-9471 Ext. 214	Clarence W. Harwood, M.D. L. Annino, R. Ph.
New Britain	Poison Control Center New Britain General Hospital 100 Grand St. 06050	224-5672	Roger T. Scully, M.D.
New Haven	Poison Control Center The Hospital of St. Raphael 1450 Chapel St. 06511	772-3900	John M. Christoforo, M.D.
	Poison Control Center Yale-New Haven Hospital 789 Howard Ave. 06504	436-1960	Thomas F. Dolan, Jr., M.D. Steven Wang, M.D.
Norwalk	Poison Control Center Norwalk Hospital 24 Stevens St. 06852	838-3611	Edward A. Rem, M.D.
Stamford	Poison Control Center Stamford Hospital Shelburne Rd. at West Broad St. 06902	327-1234 Ext. 333	Ralph A. Pesiri, M.D.

City	Name and Address	Telephone	Director and Assistant Director
(Connecticut—Continued)			
Waterbury	Poison Control Center St. Mary's Hospital 56 Franklin St. 06702	756-8351 Ext. 210	Morris Coshak, M.D. Sister Mary Lorraine, R. Ph.

DELAWARE

Wilmington	Poison Information Service 501 W. 14th St. 19899	655-3389	Elmer Fantazier, M.D. Stanley H. Weinberg

DISTRICT OF COLUMBIA

Washington	Poison Control Center Children's Hospital 13th & W Sts., N.W. 20009	835-4080 or 4081	Jose R. Puig, M.D.

FLORIDA

STATE COORDINATOR ...	Department of Health and Rehabilitative Services Jacksonville 32201	354-3961	William H. Hamlin Emergency Medical Services Program, Division of Health

City	Center	Phone	Contact
Apalachicola	Poison Control Center George E. Weems Memorial Hospital Franklin Square, Box 610 32320	653-3311	P. J. Nichols, M.D. R. B. Mabrey
Bartow	Poison Control Center Polk General Hospital 2010 E. Georgia St. P.O. Box 81 33830	533-1111 Ext. 237	J. W. Appelboom, M.D.
Bradenton	Poison Control Center Manatee Memorial Hospital 206 2nd St. 33505	746-5111 Ext. 466	Irving Hall, M.D.
Daytona Beach	Poison Control Center Halifax District Hospital Clyde Morris Blvd. 32015	255-4411 Ext. 256	Frederic Simmons, M.D.
Fort Lauderdale	Poison Control Center Broward General Hospital 1600 S. Andrews Ave. 33316	525-5411 Ext. 513	George M. Rhodes, M.D. Viola R. Mawhinney, R.N.
Fort Myers	Poison Control Center Lee Memorial Hospital U.S. Post Office Drawer 2218 33902	334-5286	Curtis R. House, M.D. R. C. McDowell, R. Ph.
Ft. Walton Beach	Poison Control Center Ft. Walton Beach Hospital 207 Hospital Dr., N.E. 32548	243-7611 Ext. 223	W. W. Thompson, M.D. Robert J. Saxer, M.D.

City	Name and Address	Telephone	Director and Assistant Director
(Florida—Continued)			
Gainesville	Poison Control Center Alachua General Hospital 315 S.W. 10th Street 32601	372-4321 Ext. 333	Sandy K. Sanders, M.D.
	Poison Information Center J. Hillis Miller Health Center University of Florida 32601	392-3591	F. L. DeBusk, M.D.
Jacksonville	Poison Control Center St. Vincent's Hospital Barrs St. & St. Johns Ave. 32204	389-7751 Ext. 315	S. P. Gyland, M.D. Ed. Marrow, M.D.
Key West	Poison Control Center Monroe General Hospital Stock Island 33040	294-3741 Ext. 237	James D. Malgrat, M.D. John Walker, R. Ph.
Lakeland	Poison Control Center Lakeland General Hospital Lakeland Hills Blvd. P.O. Box 480, 33801	686-1111 Ext. 599, 597	A. Dane Sawyer, Jr., M.D.
Leesburg	Poison Control Center Leesburg General Hospital 600 E. Dixie 32748	787-7222 Ext. 221	Paul F. Tumlin, M.D. Sharon A. Dietz, R.N.

Melbourne	Poison Control Center Brevard Hospital 1350 S. Hickory St. 32901	727-7000 Ext. 704, 741, 798	William Bourland, M.D. Glen Wagner, M.D.
Miami	Poison Control Center Jackson Memorial Hospital 1700 N.W. 10th Ave. 33136	371-9611 Ext. 378	Nancy Fawcett, M.D.
Miami Beach	Poison Control Center Mt. Sinai Hospital 4300 Alton Rd. 33140	532-3611 Ext. 3333	Robert Grayson, M.D. Milton Grossman, M.D.
Naples	Poison Control Center Naples Community Hospital 350 7th St. N. 33940	649-3131 Ext. 221	Marion Erlandson, M.D.
Ocala	Poison Control Center Munroe Memorial Hospital 1410 S. Orange St. 32670	629-7911 Ext. 15	Bobby A. Richardson, M.D.
Orlando	Poison Control Center Orange Memorial Hospital 1416 S. Orange Ave. 32806	241-2411 Ext. 656	Bruce Webster, M.D.
Panama City	Poison Control Center Memorial Hospital of Bay County 600 N. MacArthur Ave. 32401	785-7411 Ext. 652	M. M. Traxler, M.D. Bill Lowther, R.N.
Pensacola	Poison Control Center Baptist Hospital 1000 W. Moreno St. 32501	434-4811 Ext. 518, 519	John Lipsey, M.D. Vivian Whitehead, R.N.

City	Name and Address	Telephone	Director and Assistant Director
(Florida—Continued)			
Plant City	Poison Control Center South Florida Baptist Hospital Drawer H 33566	752-1188	Harold D. Brewer, M.D. Elizabeth Bell
Pompano Beach	Poison Control Center North District Hospital 201 E. Sample Rd. 33064	941-8300 Ext. 710	Robert D. Hayes, M.D. Mardis Meyer, R. Ph.
Punta Gorda	Poison Control Center Medical Center Hospital 809 E. Marion Ave. 33950	639-2191 Ext. 129	Robert H. Shedd, M.D. Faye W. Mobley, R.N.
Rockledge	Poison Control Center Wuesthoff Memorial Hospital 110 Longwood Ave. 32955	636-2211 Ext. 506, 507	T. C. Kenaston, Jr., M.D. Robert Sakolsky, M.D.
St. Petersburg	Poison Control Center Bayfront Medical Center, Inc. 701 6th St., S. 33701	894-1161 Ext. 241, 242	Donald McLanathan, M.D. D. O. Westmark, M.D.
Sarasota	Poison Control Center Sarasota Memorial Hospital 1901 Arlington Ave. 33579	955-1111 Ext. 1241	Preston Clement, Jr., M.D. Arnene Owens, R.N.

Tallahassee .... Poison Control Center
Tallahassee Memorial Hospital
N. Magnolia Dr. & Miccosukee Rd.
32303
877-2181 Ext. 299
N. T. Mustian
Ruby Goff, R.N.

Tampa .... Poison Control Center
Tampa General Hospital
Davis Islands 33606
251-6995
Sorrell Wolfson, M.D.
Martha F. Cullaro, R.N.

Titusville .... Poison Control Center
Jess Parrish Memorial Hospital
951 N. Washington Ave. 32780
269-1100 Ext. 474
Alston W. Brown, III, M.D.
Joan A. Kubasko, R.N.

West Palm Beach ... Poison Control Center
Good Samaritan Hospital
1300 N. Dixie Hwy. 33402
655-5511 Ext. 341, 342, 343
L. R. Leviton, M.D.
Rosemary Ring, R.N.

Winter Haven ...... Poison Control Center
Winter Haven Hospital, Inc.
200 Ave. F, N.E. 33880
293-1121 Ext. 222
Rita Marotti, M.D.
M. Thornhill, R.N.

GEORGIA

STATE
COORDINATOR ... Department of Public Health
Atlanta 30334
656-1839
Roger N. Justice,
Chief, Injury Control, EHS

Albany .... Poison Information Center
Phoebe Putney Memorial Hospital
417 3rd Ave., P.O. Box 1151 31705
436-5741 Ext. 155
Mack Sutton, M.D.
John Perry, R. Ph.

City	Name and Address	Telephone	Director and Assistant Director
(Georgia—Continued)			
Athens	Poison Control Center Athens General Hospital 797 Cobb St. 30601	549-9977 Ext. 223	Bill R. McKeller, R. Ph. Wayne Evans, R. Ph.
Atlanta	Poison Control Center Grady Memorial Hospital 80 Butler St., S.E. 30303	523-4711 Ext. 893	Albert Rauber, M.D. Barbara Bruner, M.D.
Augusta	Poison Information Center University Hospital University Place 30902	724-7171 Ext. 233	James W. Bennett, M.D. Agnes Roberts, R.N.
Columbus	Poison Information Center The Medical Center 19th St. & 18th Ave. 31902	324-4711 Ext. 431	Marvin D. Cohen, M.D. Daniel Sigman, M.D.
Macon	Poison Control Center Macon Hospital 777 Hemlock St. 31201	746-4113 Ext. 314, 315, 309	Shirley Scarborough, R. Ph.
Rome	Poison Control Center Floyd Hospital Turner & McCall Blvd. 30161	235-0451	James H. Williams, R. Ph. William Fricks, R. Ph.

Savannah	....	Poison Information Center Memorial Hospital Waters Ave. at 63rd St. 31404	345-3200 Ext. 367	M. E. Wilson, Jr., R. Ph. Larry Pareigis, R. Ph.
Thomasville	....	Poison Control Center John D. Archbold Memorial Hospital 900 Gordon Ave. 31792	226-4121 Ext. 209	John E. Bray, R. Ph. John M. Sisson, M.D.
Valdosta	....	Poison Control Center Pineview General Hospital Pendleton Park 31601	242-3450 Ext. 249, 250	Ronald L. Slade, R. Ph.
Waycross	....	Poison Control Center Memorial Hospital 410 Darling Ave. 31501	283-3030 Ext. 240, 241, 242	Virginia Teagler, R.N. Louise B. Trogdon, R.N.

GUAM

| COORDINATOR | ... | Department of Public Health and Social Services Agana 96910 | 42-4158 | Joseph H. Gerber, M.D. |
| Agana | .... | Poison Control Center Guam Memorial Hospital 96910 | 746-9171 | Antonio T. Cruz, R. Ph. Brihida C. Aguigui, R.N. |

HAWAII

| STATE COORDINATOR | ... | Department of Health Honolulu 96801 | 531-7776 | David D. Holaday, M.D. Chief, Injury Control Branch |

City	Name and Address	Telephone	Director and Assistant Director
(Hawaii—Continued)			
Honolulu	Poison Control Center Kauikeolani Children's Hospital 226 North Kuakini St. 96817	531-3511	Richard K. B. Ho, M.D. Ross Hagino, M.D.

IDAHO

City	Name and Address	Telephone	Director and Assistant Director
STATE COORDINATOR	State Department of Health Boise, 83701	384-2494	W. W. Benson Poison Control Coordinator
Boise	Poison Information Center St. Luke's Hospital Pharmacy 130 E. Bannock 83702	342-7781	Donald J. Ness, R. Ph. Brent Fricke, R. Ph.

ILLINOIS

City	Name and Address	Telephone	Director and Assistant Director
STATE COORDINATOR	Department of Public Health Springfield 62706	525-7747	Norman J. Rose, M.D. Bureau of Hazardous Substances and Poison Control

Aurora	Poison Control Center Copley Memorial Hospital Lincoln & Weston Aves. 60507	896-4611 Ext. 725	Ruby Barnes, R.N.
	Poison Control Center St. Charles Hospital 400 E. New York St. 60507	897-8714 Ext. 50	Sister M. Alberta, R. Ph.
Belleville	Poison Control Center Memorial Hospital 4501 N. Park Dr. 62223	233-7750 Ext. 250, 251	H. L. Lange, M.D.
Belvidere	Poison Control Center Highland Hospital 1625 S. State St. 61008	547-5441 Ext. 367	Paul Dommers, M.D.
Berwyn	Poison Control Center MacNeal Memorial Hospital 3249 Oak Park Ave. 60402	484-2211 Ext. 311, 312, 314	Ronald B. Mack, M.D.
Bloomington	Poison Control Center Mennonite Hospital 807 N. Main 61701	828-5241 Ext. 311	William Dunn
	Poison Control Center St. Joseph Hospital 2200 E. Washington 61701	829-9481 Ext. 352, 354	Edward P. Wood, M.D.
Cairo	Poison Control Center St. Mary's Hospital 2020 Cedar St. 62914	734-2400 Ext. 42 Night: 45	Emma Womble, R.N.

City	Name and Address	Telephone	Director and Assistant Director
(Illinois—Continued)			
Canton	Poison Control Center Graham Hospital Association 210 W. Walnut St. 61520	647–5240 Ext. 230	Gary J. Keifer, R. Ph.
Carbondale	Poison Control Center Doctors Memorial Hospital 404 W. Main St. 62901	457–4101	Homer H. Hanson, M.D.
Carthage	Poison Control Center Memorial Hospital End S. Adams St. 62321	357–3133 Ext. 57	Lois Gorby, R.N.
Centralia	Poison Control Center St. Mary's Hospital 400 N. Pleasant Ave. 62801	532–6731 Ext. 626 Night: 629	W. W. Davidson, M.D.
Champaign	Poison Control Center Burnham City Hospital 311 E. Stoughton St. 61820	337–2533	Miss Boston, R.N.
Chanute AFB	Poison Control Center USAF Hospital Chanute Air Force Base 61866 (Limited to treatment of military	495–3133 495–3134	Charles S. Brummer, Captain

		(personnel and families, except for indicated civilian emergencies)		
Chicago	Chicago Master Center Presbyterian–St. Lukes Hospital 1753 W. Congress Parkway 60612	942–5969	Joseph R. Christian, M.D.
Chester	Poison Control Center Memorial Hospital 1900 State St. 62233	826–2388 Ext. 44	Milton J. Zemlyn, M.D.
Danville	Poison Control Center Lake View Memorial Hospital 812 N. Logan Ave. 61832	443–5221	Megan Tanner, M.D.
	Poison Control Center St. Elizabeth Hospital 600 Sager Ave. 61832	442–6300	W. Robert Elghammer, M.D.
Decatur	Poison Control Center Decatur Memorial Hospital 2300 N. Edward St. 62526	877–8121 Ext. 676, 675	Warren Mann, R. Ph.
	Poison Control Center St. Mary's Hospital 1800 E. Lake Shore Dr. 62525	429–2966 Ext. 640	Frances Dare, R.N.
Des Plaines	Poison Control Center Holy Family Hospital 100 N. River Rd. 60016	299–2281 Ext. 856	Richard Repasy, M.D.

City	Name and Address	Telephone	Director and Assistant Director
(Illinois—Continued)			
East St. Louis	Poison Control Center Christian Welfare Hospital 1509 Illinois Ave. 62201	874-7076 Ext. 232	Richard D. Osland, M.D.
	Poison Control Center St. Mary's Hospital 129 N. 8th St. 62201	274-1900 Ext. 204	Joseph W. Compton, M.D.
Effingham	Poison Control Center St. Anthony's Memorial Hospital 503 N. Maple 62401	342-2121 Ext. 67	Rose Mary Niebrugge, R.N.
Elgin	Poison Control Center St. Joseph's Hospital 277 Jefferson Ave. 60120	741-5400 Ext. 65-69	Andrew J. Nowakowski, M.D.
	Poison Control Center Sherman Hospital 934 Center St. 60120	742-9800 Ext. 682	Lucille Carey, R.N.
Elmhurst	Poison Control Center Memorial Hospital of DuPage County 315 Schiller St. 60127	833-1400 Ext. 551, 552	Mary E. Reedy, M.D., Attn: Leonard C. Klemme, Chief Pharmacist

Evanston	Poison Control Center Community Hospital 2040 Brown Ave. 60201	869-5400 Ext. 54 Night: 58	Jacob A. Frye, M.D.
	Poison Control Center Evanston Hospital 2650 Ridge Ave. 60201	492-0460	Robert A. McGuigan, M.D.
	Poison Control Center St. Francis Hospital 355 Ridge Ave. 60202	492-2440	Lolita C. Dour, R.N.
Evergreen Park	Poison Control Center Little Company of Mary Hospital 2800 W. 95th St. 60642	422-6200 HI 5-6000 Ext. 221	Ralph Spaeth, M.D. Joseph V. Arnold, R. Ph.
Fairbury	Poison Control Center Fairbury Hospital 519 S. 5th St. 61739	692-2346	Dorothy Yoder, R.N.
Freeport	Poison Control Center Freeport Memorial Hospital 420 S. Harlem 61032	233-4131 Ext. 228	Philip Wachtel, M.D.
Galena	Poison Control Center The Galena Hospital District Summit St. 61036	777-1340	Thomas Reed
Galesburg	Poison Control Center Galesburg Cottage Hospital 674 N. Seminary St. 61401	343-4121 Ext. 356	Donald L. Grieme, M.D.

City	Name and Address	Telephone	Director and Assistant Director
(Illinois—Continued)			
Galesburg	Poison Control Center St. Mary's Hospital 239 S. Cherry St. 61401	343–8161 Ext. 210	Homer L. Fleisher, Jr., M.D.
Granite City	Poison Control Center St. Elizabeth Hospital 2100 Madison Ave. 62040	876–2020 Ext. 224	Sister Mary Benedict, R. Ph.
Harvey	Poison Control Center Ingalls Memorial Hospital 15510 Page Ave. 60426	333–2300 Ext. 787, 792	Raymond E. Lesser, M.D.
Highland	Poison Control Center St. Joseph Hospital 1515 Main St. 62249	654–2171 Ext. 243	Edna Zobrist, R.N.
Highland Park	Poison Control Center Highland Park Hospital Foundation 718 Glenview Ave. 60035	432–8000 Ext. 561, 562, 563	Burton Green, M.D.
Hinsdale	Poison Control Center Hinsdale Sanitarium & Hospital 120 N. Oak St. 60521	323–2100 Ext. 336	F. W. Tracy, M.D.

Hoopeston	Poison Control Center Hoopeston Community Memorial Hospital 701 E. Orange 60942	283-5531	T. S. Strzembosz, M.D.
Jacksonville	Poison Control Center Passavant Memorial Area Hospital 1600 W. Walnut St. 62650	245-9541 Ext. 222	Joseph Kozma, M.D.
Joliet	Poison Control Center St. Joseph's Hospital 333 N. Madison St. 60435	725-7133 Ext. 793	William Frescura, R. Ph.
	Poison Control Center Silver Cross Hospital 600 Walnut St. 60432	727-1711 Ext. 731, 780, 679, 680	Arlene Doyer, R.N.
Kankakee	Poison Control Center Riverside Hospital 350 N. Wall St. 60901	933-1671 Ext. 606	Andrew P. Adams, M.D.
	Poison Control Center St. Mary's Hospital 150 S. Fifth Ave. 60901	939-4111 Ext. 735	A. A. Palow, M.D.
Kewanee	Poison Control Center Kewanee Public Hospital 719 Elliott St. 61443	853-3361 Ext. 219	Richard M. Terry, M.D.

City	Name and Address	Telephone	Director and Assistant Director
(Illinois—Continued)			
Lake Forest	Poison Control Center Lake Forest Hospital 660 Northwestmoreland Road 60045	234-5600 Ext. 608	Gerald Lasin, M.D.
LaSalle	Poison Control Center St. Mary's Hospital 1015 O'Conor Ave. 61301	223-0607	E. Fesco, M.D.
Libertyville	Poison Control Center Condell Memorial Hospital Cleveland & Stewart Aves. 60048	362-2900 Ext. 325, 326	Richard R. Vevle
Lincoln	Poison Control Center Abraham Lincoln Memorial Hospital 315 Eighth St. 62656	732-2161 Ext. 346	R. Lynn Ijams, M.D.
McHenry	Poison Control Center McHenry Hospital 3516 W. Waukegan Rd. 60050	385-2200 Ext. 614	Peter Griesbach, M.D.
Macomb	Poison Control Center McDonough District Hospital 525 E. Grant St. 61455	833-4101	J. L. Symmonds, M.D.

Mattoon	Poison Control Center Memorial Hospital District of Coles County 2101 Champaign Ave. 61938	234–8881 Ext. 43 Night: 29	William F. Wuenscher, R. Ph.
Maywood	Poison Control Center Loyola University Hospital 2160 S. 1st Ave. 60153	531–3886	Eugene F. Diamond, M.D.
Melrose Park	Poison Control Center Westlake Hospital 1225 Superior St. 60160	681–3000 Ext. 226, 239	Erast Burachynskyj, M.D.
Mendota	Poison Control Center Mendota Community Hospital Memorial Dr. 61342	7461 Ext. 20	James R. Durham, M.D.
Moline	Poison Control Center Moline Public Hospital 635 10th Ave. 61265	762–8651 Ext. 232	R. Kaplan, M.D.
Monmouth	Poison Control Center Community Memorial Hospital West Harlem Ave. 61462	734–3141 Ext. 224	Wendell Roller, M.D.
Mt. Carmel	Poison Control Center Wabash General Hospital 1418 College Dr. 62863	262–4121 Ext. 231	T. R. Young, M.D.
Mt. Vernon	Poison Control Center Good Samaritan Hospital 605 N. 12th St. 62864	242–4600 Ext. 303	Alan W. Anderson, M.D. Sister M. Henrietta, R.N.

City	Name and Address	Telephone	Director and Assistant Director
(Illinois—Continued)			
Naperville	Poison Control Center Edward Hospital S. Washington St. 60540	355–0450 Ext. 326	Arthur Smid, M.D.
Normal	Poison Control Center Brokaw Hospital Franklin & Virginia Ave. 61761	829–7685 Ext. 274	Thelma Atkinson, R.N.
Oak Lawn	Poison Control Center Christ Community Hospital 4440 W. 95th St. 60453	423–7000 Ext. 659, 660, 661	Silvio Morales, M.D.
Oak Park	Poison Control Center W. Suburban Hospital 518 N. Austin Blvd. 60302	383–6200 Ext. 6747	Peter Baker, M.D.
Olney	Poison Control Center Richland Memorial Hospital 800 E. Locust St. 62450	395–2131	John D. Stull, M.D.
Ottawa	Poison Control Center Ryburn Memorial Hospital 701 Clinton St. 61350	433–3100	G. Alan Neufeld, M.D.

Park Ridge	Poison Control Center Lutheran General Hospital 1775 Dempster St. 60068	692-2210 Ext. 1220 Night: 1460	Adolph Sattler, M.D.
Pekin	Poison Control Center Pekin Memorial Hospital 14th & Court 61554	347-1151 Ext. 233, 241	Margaret M. Torrey, M.D.
Peoria	Poison Control Center Methodist Hospital 221 N.E. Glen Oak Ave. 61603	685-6511 Ext. 250	
	Poison Control Center Proctor Community Hospital 5409 N. Knoxville 61614	691-4702 Ext. 791, 792	Carleton R. Smith, M.D.
	Poison Control Center St. Francis Hospital 530 N.E. Glen Oak Ave. 61603	674-2943	Ronald Pechan
Peru	Poison Control Center Peoples Hospital 925 W St. 61354	223-3300 Ext. 55 Night: 40	Susan Duncan, R.N.
Pittsfield	Poison Control Center Illini Community Hospital 640 W. Washington St. 62363	285-2115 Ext. 238 Night: 213	Warren C. Barrow, M.D.
Princeton	Poison Control Center Perry Memorial Hospital 530 E. Park Ave. 61356	875-2811 Ext. 311	J. L. Foresman, M.D. S. S. Frank, M.D.

City	Name and Address	Telephone	Director and Assistant Director
(Illinois—Continued)			
Quincy	Poison Control Center Blessing Hospital 1005 Broadway 62301	223–5811 Ext. 211, 212	Leora Forquer, R.N.
	Poison Control Center St. Mary's Hospital 1415 Vermont St. 62301	223–1200 Ext. 275	Walter M. Whitaker, M.D.
Rockford	Poison Control Center Rockford Memorial Hospital 2400 N. Rockton Ave. 61103	968–6861 Ext. 441	Keith Wrage, M.D.
	Poison Control Center St. Anthony's Hospital 5666 E. State St. 61108	226–2041	Joyce Wilkins, R.N.
	Poison Control Center Swedish-American Hospital 1316 Charles St. 61108	968–6898 Ext. 602	Floy Omark, R.N.
Rock Island	Poison Control Center St. Anthony's Hospital 767 30th St. 61202	788–7631 Ext. 771, 772	William Kalman

St. Charles	Poison Control Center Delnor Hospital 975 N. Fifth Ave. 60174	584-3300 Ext. 229, 218 Night: 286	R. R. Grayson, M.D.
Scott Air Force Base .	Poison Control Center USAF Medical Center 62225	256-7595	Col. Kenneth S. Shepard, MC
Springfield	Poison Control Center Memorial Hospital 1st & Miller Sts. 62701	528-2041 Ext. 333	W. Edward Quarry, R.N.
	Poison Control Center St. John's Hospital 701 E. Mason St. 62701	544-6451 Ext. 375	Sister M. Kathleen, R.N.
Streator	Poison Control Center St. Mary's Hospital 111 E. Spring St. 61364	672-3189 Ext. 221	H. A. Hengen, M.D.
Urbana	Poison Control Center Carle Foundation Hospital 611 W. Park St. 61801	337-3313	Leo G. Perucca, M.D.
	Poison Control Center Mercy Hospital 1400 W. Park Ave. 61801	337-2131	Alan Buntain, R. Ph.
Waukegan	Poison Control Center St. Therese Hospital W. Waukegan St. 60085	688-6470 688-6471	Max Z. Cahan, M.D.

City	Name and Address	Telephone	Director and Assistant Director
(Illinois—Continued)			
Waukegan	Poison Control Center Victory Memorial Hospital 1324 N. Sheridan Rd. 60085	688-4181	J. DeRyke, R.N.
Woodstock	Poison Control Center Memorial Hospital for McHenry County 527 W. South St. 60098	338-2500 Ext. 32	Richard Keller, R. Ph.
Zion	Poison Control Center Zion-Benton Hospital 2500 Emmaus Ave. 60099	872-4561 Ext. 240	Adolph Berke, M.D.

INDIANA

City	Name and Address	Telephone	Director and Assistant Director
STATE COORDINATOR ...	State Board of Health Indianapolis 46206	633-5490	A. C. Offutt, M.D. State Health Commissioner Robert J. Murray, Chief Hazardous Products Section Division of Drug Control

Anderson	Poison Control Center St. John's Hickey Memorial Hospital 2015 Jackson St. 46014	694–2511 Ext. 251	Thomas J. Schroeder, R. Ph.
Angola	Poison Control Center Cameron Memorial Hospital, Inc. 416 E. Maumee St. 46703	665–2141 Ext. 42 665–2166	Irene F. Kenyon, R.N. Max White, R. Ph.
East Chicago	Poison Control Center St. Catherine Hospital 4321 Fir St. 46312	EX 7–3080	Edward Broomes, M.D. S. G. Zallen, M.D.
Elkhart	Poison Control Center Elkhart General Hospital 600 E. Blvd. 46514	523–5350 Ext. 215	C. Richard Yoder, M.D.
Evansville	Poison Control Center Deaconess Hospital 600 Mary St. 47710	426–3405	Robert E. Arendell, M.D.
	Poison Control Center St. Mary's Hospital 3700 Washington Ave. 47715	477–6261	Julian D. Present, M.D.
	Poison Control Center Welborn Memorial Baptist Hospital 412 S.E. 4th St. 47713	423–3103 Ext. 336 Night: 253	Charles L. Warner, M.D. Richard F. Emig, R. Ph.

City	Name and Address	Telephone	Director and Assistant Director
(Indiana—Continued)			
Fort Wayne	Poison Control Center Parkview Memorial Hospital 220 Randalia Dr. 46805	484-6636 Ext. 530	William O. Wissman, R. Ph. Grace Kammeyer, R.N.
	Poison Control Center St. Joseph's Hospital 700 Broadway 46802	742-4121 Ext. 211	Gerri L. Heck, R.N. J. L. Lawrence, R.N.
Frankfort	Poison Control Center Clinton County Hospital 1300 S. Jackson St. 46041	654-4451	Frederick W. Flora, M.D.
Gary	Poison Control Center Methodist Hospital of Gary, Inc. 600 Grant St. 46402	882-9461 Ext. 709	John Sabo, R. Ph. Patricia Sikich, R.N.
Goshen	Poison Control Center Goshen General Hospital 200 High Park Ave. 46526	533-2141 Ext. 462	C. P. Duren, M.D.
Hammond	Poison Control Center St. Margaret Hospital 25 Douglas St. 46320	WE 2-2300 Ext. 700	Herbert I. Arbeiter, M.D. V. Shirey, R.N.

Indianapolis	Poison Control Center Marion County General Hospital 960 Locke St. 46202	630–7351	John D. Miller, M.D. Arvine G. Popplewell, M.D.
	Poison Control Center Methodist Hospital of Indiana, Inc. 1604 N. Capitol Ave. 46202	924–8355	Maxine J. Bush, R.N. Marjorie Farmer, R.N.
Kokomo	Poison Control Center Howard Community Hospital 3500 S. La Fountain St. 46901	453–0702 Ext. 218	
Lafayette	Poison Control Center Purdue University Student Health Center 47907	749–2441 Ext. 245	L. W. Combs, M.D. Joanne Quendling, R.N.
	Poison Control Center St. Elizabeth Hospital 1501 Hartford St. 47904	742–0221 Ext. 428, 421	Barbara Oldfield, R.N.
La Grange	Poison Control Center La Grange County Hospital Route 1 46761	463–2144 Ext. 34	Allen S. Martin, M.D. Merle S. Rawson
Lebanon	Poison Control Center Witham Memorial Hospital 1124 N. Lebanon St. 46052	482–2700 Ext. 44	Thomas Dillon, M.D. B. Martz, R.N.

City	Name and Address	Telephone	Director and Assistant Director
(Indiana—Continued)			
Madison	Poison Control Center King's Daughters' Hospital 112 Presbyterian Ave. P.O. Box 447 47250	265-5211 Ext. 14	Jean Grimsley, R.N.
Marion	Poison Control Center Marion General Hospital Wabash & Euclid Ave. 46952	662-1441 Ext. 294, 295	Mirhan Boldy, M.D.
Mishawaka	Poison Control Center St. Joseph Hospital 215 W. 4th St. 46544	259-2431	
Muncie	Poison Control Center Ball Memorial Hospital 2401 University Ave. 47303	284-9371 Ext. 241, 242, 371	Junia L. Rice, R.N.
Portland	Poison Control Center Jay County Hospital 505 W. Arch St. 47371	726-7131 Ext. 159	F. E. Keeling, M.D. Ivan E. Clear, R. Ph.
Richmond	Poison Control Center Reid Memorial Hospital 1401 Chester Blvd. 47374	962-4545 Ext. 222, 333	Olin K. Wiland, M.D. Jessie Snyder, R.N.

Shelbyville .... Poison Control Center
William S. Major Hospital
150 W. Washington St. 46176

392-3211
Ext. 52

Carolyn Rosenfeld, R.N.
Zoe Scripture, R.N.

South Bend .... Poison Control Center
Memorial Hospital of South Bend
615 Michigan St. 46601

234-9041
Ext. 258,
259

Norma J. Schafer, R.N.
William B. Frey, M.D.

Poison Control Center
St. Joseph's Hospital
811 E. Madison St. 46622

234-2151
Ext. 264

Bernard Vagner, M.D.

Terre Haute .... Poison Control Center
Union Hospital, Inc.
1606 N. 7th St. 47804

232-0361
Ext. 229

Roger F. West, M.D.
Sylvia Alexander, R.N.

IOWA

STATE
COORDINATOR ... Department of Health
Des Moines 50319

281-5787

Paul H. Ogilvie, Division of
Maternal & Child Health

Des Moines .... Poison Information Center
Raymond Blank Memorial Hospital
1200 Pleasant St. 50308

283-6254

Mark Thoman, M.D.

Fort Dodge .... Poison Information Center
Bethesda General Hospital
Lutheran Park Rd. 50501

573-3101
Ext. 230

Donald E. Tyler, M.D.
Robert Bellinger, R. Ph.

Iowa City .... Poison Information Center
University Hospital
Pharmacy Department 52241

356-1616

D. L. Dunphy, M.D.
R. W. Dick, R. Ph.

City	Name and Address	Telephone	Director and Assistant Director
	KANSAS		
STATE COORDINATOR	State Department of Health Topeka 66612	296-8708	Evan Wright, Director Food and Drug Division
Atchison	Poison Control Center Atchison Hospital 1301 N. 2nd St. 66002	EM 7-2131 Ext. 28	Ira M. Morrison, M.D.
Dodge City	Poison Control Center Trinity Hospital 1107 6th St. 67801	227-8133	Robert D. Boles, M.D. Mrs. Vesta Palmer, R.N.
Emporia	Poison Control Center Newman Memorial Hospital 12th & Chestnut Sts. 66801	342-7120 Ext. 330	David R. Davis, M.D.
Fort Scott	Poison Control Center Mercy Hospital 821 Burke St. 66701	BA 3-2200 Ext. 52	Gary F. Crabtree, R. Ph. Jo Coiner, R.N.
Great Bend	Poison Control Center Central Kansas Medical Center 3515 Broadway 67530	792-2511 Ext. 115	David Shivel, M.D. Sister Lois Crotinger, R.N.

Hays	Poison Control Center Hadley Memorial Hospital 201 E. 7th St. 67601	625-3441	Kent Atkins, R. Ph.
Kansas City	Poison Control Center University of Kansas Medical Center, Department of Pharmacology Rainbow Blvd. at 39th St. 66103	AD 6-5252 Ext. 555	John Doull, M.D. William Sosnow, M.D.
Lawrence	Poison Control Center Lawrence Memorial Hospital 325 Maine St. 66044	843-3680 Ext. 362	Vernon Branson, M.D.
Parsons	Poison Control Center Labette County Medical Center South 21st St. 67357	421-4880 Ext. 245	John P. White, M.D. Darrel R. Miner, R. Ph.
Salina	Poison Control Center St. John's Hospital 139 N. Penn St. 67401	TA 7-5591 Ext. 125	William Null, M.D. Sister Edna Louise, R.N.
Topeka	Poison Control Center Stormont-Vail Hospital 10th & Washburn Sts. 66604	234-9961 Ext. 150	
	Poison Information Center State Department of Health State Office Bldg. Topeka Ave. at 10th 66612	296-3708	Evan Wright

City	Name and Address	Telephone	Director and Assistant Director
(Kansas—Continued)			
Wichita	Poison Control Center Wesley Hospital Medical Library 550 N. Hillside Ave. 67214	685–2151 Ext. 377	R. A. Nelson, M.D.

KENTUCKY

City	Name and Address	Telephone	Director and Assistant Director
STATE COORDINATOR ...	State Department of Health Frankfort 40601	564–4830	Lester Chadwell Division of Health
Ashland	Poison Control Center King's Daughters' Hospital 2201 Lexington Ave. 41101	325–7755 Ext. 291	Harry Phaff, R. Ph.
Fort Thomas	Poison Control Center St. Luke Hospital 85 N. Grand Ave. 41075	441–6100 Ext. 215, 216	Paul J. Vaal, R. Ph.
Lexington	Poison Control Center Central Baptist Hospital 1740 S. Limestone St. 40503	278–3411 Ext. 152, 153	Carl E. Beck, R. Ph.

			Charles A. Walton, R. Ph. Gerald P. Sherman, R. Ph.

Poison Information Center
University of Kentucky Medical
Center 40506 — 233-5853 — Charles A. Walton, R. Ph. / Gerald P. Sherman, R. Ph.

Owensboro .... Poison Control Center
Owensboro-Daviess County Hospital
811 Hospital Court 42301 — 683-3513
Ext. 275 — Bill W. McKnight, R. Ph. / H. L. Abell, R. Ph.

Paducah .... Poison Control Center
Western Baptist Hospital
2501 Kentucky Ave. 42001 — 444-6361
Ext. 221 — Victor Wallace, R. Ph.

LOUISIANA

STATE
COORDINATOR ... State Department of Health
New Orleans 70160 — 527-5822 — Milton E. Kossack, Head
Division of Public Health
Education

Bogalusa .... Poison Information Center
Washington–St. Tammany Charity
Hospital
400 Memphis St. 70427 — 735-1322 — Leroy Branch, M.D. / L. Paraguya, M.D.

Monroe .... Poison Control Center
St. Francis Hospital
309 Jackson St. 71201 — 325-6454 — J. Bolling Jones, M.D. / John Guerriero, Jr., R. Ph.

New Orleans ...... Louisiana Poison Control Center of
New Orleans
U.S. Public Health Service Hospital
210 State St. 70118 — 899-3409 — I. M. Perret, Jr., M.D. / Francis X. O'Sullivan, R. Ph.

City	Name and Address	Telephone	Director and Assistant Director
(Louisiana—Continued)			
Shreveport	Poison Control Center T. E. Schumpert Memorial Hospital 915 Margaret Place 71101	422–0709 424–6411 Ext. 240, 271	Harold B. Levy, M.D.

MAINE

STATE COORDINATOR ...	Department of Health & Welfare Augusta 04330	289–2736	Dean H. Fisher, M.D. Commissioner
Togus	Poison Control Center Veterans Administration Center Kennebec County 04330	623–8411 Ext. 283 305	Robert L. Ohler, M.D.

MARYLAND

STATE COORDINATOR ...	State Department of Health Baltimore 21201	382–2668	John L. Pitts, M.D., Chief Division of Maternal and Child Health
Annapolis	Poison Control Center Anne Arundel General Hospital Franklin & Cathedral Sts. 21401	268–4444 Ext. 277	Charles W. Stahl, R. Ph.

Baltimore	Poison Information Center Baltimore City Hospital 4940 Eastern Ave. 21224	DI 2-0800	Marv Stang Furth, M.D.
	Poison Control Center Johns Hopkins Hospital 601 N. Broadway 21205	955-6371	Neil Sims, M.D. Robert S. Thompson, M.D.
	Poison Control Center University of Maryland Hospital Redwood & Greene Sts. 21201	955-7592 Night: 955-8761	Chief Pediatric Resident
Bethesda	Poison Control Center Suburban Hospital Emergency Room 8600 Old Georgetown Rd. 20014	530-3880	Charles Savarese, M.D. Evelyn F. Birdwell, R.N.
Cumberland	Tri-State Poison Control Center Sacred Heart Hospital 900 Seton Dr. 21401	729-5200	Gina M. Glick, M.D. Rose M. Miller, R.N.
Easton	Poison Control Center Memorial Hospital S. Washington St. 21601	822-5555	William E. Jaffe, R. Ph.
Hagerstown	Poison Control Center Washington County Hospital King & Antietam Sts. 21740	733-3000	A. M. Bacon, Jr., M.D. Max Byrkit, M.D.
Silver Spring	Poison Control Center Holy Cross Hospital Forest Glen Road 20910	495-1225	Charles Savarese, M.D. T. Coleman, M.D.

MASSACHUSETTS

City	Name and Address	Telephone	Director and Assistant Director
STATE COORDINATOR	State Department of Public Health Boston 02133	727-2700	Alfred L. Frechette, M.D. Commissioner of Public Health
Boston	Poison Information Center Children's Medical Center 300 Longwood Ave. 02115	232-2120	Joel J. Alpert, M.D.
Fall River	Poison Control Center Union Hospital 300 Hanover St. 02720	679-6405 Ext. 232	Roger L. LeMaire, M.D.
New Bedford	Poison Control Center St. Luke's Hospital 52 Brigham St. 02740	997-1515 Ext. 311	William R. Collins, M.D. Kay Mahoney, R.N.
Springfield	Poison Control Center Mercy Hospital 233 Carew St. 01104	788-7321 Ext. 229	Joseph R. Stirlacci, M.D. Carl W. Janovsky, M.D.
	Poison Control Center Springfield Hospital Medical Center 759 Chestnut St. 01107	787-3200 Ext. 3233	Leandre Giguere, M.D.

	Poison Control Center Wesson Memorial Hospital 140 High St. 01105	ST 5-1241 Ext. 218	John P. Sigsbee, M.D. L. Liszka, R.N.
Worcester	Poison Information Center Worcester City Hospital 26 Queen St. 01610	799-7094	Arnold Gurwitz, M.D. Grace Carney, R.N.

MICHIGAN

STATE COORDINATOR ...	Department of Public Health Lansing 48914	373-1320	Douglas H. Fryer, M.D. Chief, Developmental Service
Adrian	Poison Control Center Emma L. Bixby Hospital 818 Riverside Ave. 49221	265-6161	Robert Greiner, M.D. Thomas Arnold, R. Ph.
Ann Arbor	Poison Control Center University of Michigan Medical Center 48104	764-5102	Patricia O'Connor, M.D. Owen Haig, M.D.
Battle Creek	Poison Control Center Community Hospital 200 Tomkins St. 49016	Woodward 3-5521	Metta Lou Henderson, R. Ph.
Bay City	Poison Control Center Mercy Hospital 100 15th St. 48706	Twinbrook 5-8511	Frederick Meyer, R. Ph.
Berrien Center	Poison Control Center Berrien General Hospital Dean's Hill Rd. 49102	471-7761	Richard C. Chaudoir, R. Ph.

City	Name and Address	Telephone	Director and Assistant Director
(Michigan—Continued)			
Coldwater	Poison Control Center Community Health Center of Branch County 274 E. Chicago St. 49036	279–9501	John C. Heffelfinger, M.D.
Detroit	Poison Control Center Children's Hospital 5224 St. Antoine St. 48202	833–1000	Paul V. Wooley, Jr., M.D. Regine Aronow, M.D.
	Poison Information Center City Health Department 1151 Taylor Ave. 48202	TR 2–1540	William G. Frederick, Sc.D. William Lenz, M.D.
	Poison Control Center Mount Carmel Mercy Hospital 6071 W. Outer Dr. 48235	864–5400	John Moses, M.D. Forrest P. Becker, R. Ph.
Eloise	Poison Control Center Wayne County General Hospital 30712 Michigan Ave. 48132	722–2500 Ext. 6230, 6231	Kenneth Vaughn, M.D. Gerald A. Rigg, M.D.
Flint	Poison Control Center Hurley Hospital 6th Ave. & Begole 48502	Cedar 2–1161	William Nichols, M.D. Douglas H. Vivian, R. Ph.

Grand Rapids	Poison Control Center Blodgett Memorial Hospital 1840 Wealthy, S.E. 49506	456-5301	John P. Foxworthy, M.D. Donald Ekdom, R. Ph.
	Poison Control Center Butterworth Hospital 100 Michigan, N.E. 49503	451-3591	John R. Wilson, M.D.
	Poison Control Center Grand Rapids Osteopathic Hospital 1919 Boston Street, S.E. 49506	452-5151	Eugene M. Johnson, D.O. Oliver Gysin, R. Ph.
	Poison Control Center St. Mary's Hospital 201 Lafayette, S.E. 49503	459-3131	Wallace Duffin, M.D. Myrtle McLain, M.D.
Hancock ··········	Poison Control Center St. Joseph's Hospital 200 Michigan Ave. 49930	482-1122	Howard E. Otto, M.D. Sr. Mary Sharon Jones, R. Ph.
Kalamazoo ········	Poison Control Center Bronson Methodist Hospital 252 E. Lovell St. 49006	342-9821	H. Sidney Heersma, M.D. Kenneth Huckendubler, R. Ph.
Lansing ··········	Poison Control Center St. Lawrence Hospital 1210 W. Saginaw St. 48914	372-3610	Howard Comstock, M.D. Richard Campbell, R. Ph.
Marquette ········	Poison Control Center St. Luke's Hospital W. College Ave. 49855	Canal 6-3551	Norman Matthews, M.D. Tom Finlan, R. Ph.

City	Name and Address	Telephone	Director and Assistant Director
(Michigan—Continued)			
Midland	Poison Control Center Midland Hospital 4005 Orchard Dr. 48640	TE 5–6711	K. W. Linsenmann, M.D. Mrs. Anne Gagne, R.N.
Monroe	Poison Control Center Memorial Hospital of Monroe 700 Stewart Rd. 48161	CH 1–6500	Donald Wojack, R. Ph.
Petoskey	Poison Control Center Little Traverse Hospital 416 Connable 49770	Diamond 7–2551	James M. Stamm, R. Ph.
Pontiac	Poison Control Center St. Joseph Mercy Hospital 900 Woodward Ave. 48053	338–9111	Robert J. Mason, M.D.
Port Huron	Poison Control Center Mercy Hospital 2601 Electric Ave. 48060	Yukon 5–9531	Robert Lugg, M.D.
Saginaw	Poison Control Center Saginaw General Hospital 1447 N. Harrison Rd. 48602	753–3411	Wm. G. Mason, M.D. Dale Schultz, R. Ph.

| Traverse City | .... | Poison Control Center
Munson Medical Center
Traverse City 49684 | 9,17–6140 | Philip K. Wiley, M.D.
A. McCrackin, R. Ph. |

MINNESOTA

STATE COORDINATOR	...	State Department of Health Minneapolis 55440	378–1150	Warren R. Lawson, M.D. Director, Poison Information Center
Bemidji	....	Poison Information Center Bemidji Hospital 56601	751–5430 Ext. 40	Joel T. Deweese, M.D.
Brainerd	....	Poison Information Center St. Joseph's Hospital 56401	829–2861	William O. McLane, M.D.
Crookston	....	Poison Information Center Riverview Hospital 56716	281–4682 Ext. 250	Robert F. Schnabel, M.D. Mrs. Mernie Gredvig
Duluth	....	Poison Information Center St. Luke's Hospital 55805	727–6636 Ext. 211	E. I. Parson, M.D. H. Fisketti, M.D.
		Poison Information Center St. Mary's Hospital 407 E. 3rd St. 55805	727–4551 Ext. 359 Night: 291	H. H. Reed, M.D. Richard L. Kienzle, R. Ph.
Fergus Falls	....	Poison Information Center Lake Region Hospital 56537	736–5475 Ext. 222	Glenn Mouritsen, M.D.
Fridley	....	Poison Information Center Unity Hospital 550 Osborne Rd. 55432	786–2200 Ext. 221, 222, 223	Steve Kachina, R. Ph. Jean Johnson, R.N.

City	Name and Address	Telephone	Director and Assistant Director
(Minnesota—Continued)			
Mankato	Poison Information Center Immanuel–St. Joseph's Hospital 325 Garden Blvd. 56001	387–1851	J. C. Norris, M.D. Roland Marshall, R. Ph.
Marshall	Poison Information Center Louis Weiner Memorial Hospital 56258	532–2263 Sta. 31	William M. Kaczrowski, M.D. L. E. Stover, M.D.
Minneapolis	Fairview Hospital 2312 South 6th Street 55406	332–0282 Ext. 313	L. B. Folsom, M.D. Donald Amatuzid, M.D.
	Hennepin County General Hospital 620 S. 6th Street 55415	330–3930	Richard B. Raile, M.D. Hildred Prose, R.N.
	Poison Information Center Minnesota Department of Health 717 Delaware St. S.E. 55440	378–1150 Ext. 352 Night: 929–6491 784–1869	Warren R. Lawson, M.D. Bruce S. Olson Dr. Lawson Mr. Olson
	North Memorial Hospital 3220 Lowry Ave. N. 55422	588–0616 Ext. 342	Saburo Aisawa, R. Ph. Duane Nelson, R. Ph.
	Northwestern Hospital 810 E. 27th St. 55407	332–7266	A. J. Schroeder, M.D.

Morris	Poison Information Center Stevens County Memorial Hospital 56267	589–1313 Sta. 1	William J. Kozel, M.D. Irene Finstad, R.N.
Rochester	Poison Information Center Rochester Methodist Hospital 55901	282–4461 Ext. 5250	Earl A. Schwerman, R. Ph. Edward Mansfield, R. Ph.
St. Cloud	Poison Information Center St. Cloud Hospital 56301	251–2700 Ext. 151, 152 Night: 221	R. A. Murray, M.D. Lawrence F. Olson, R. Ph.
St. Paul	Poison Information Center Bethesda Lutheran Hospital 559 Capitol Blvd. 55101	227–8611 Ext. 301	Kenneth Peterson, M.D. Mrs. Margaret Kehr, R.N.
	Children's Hospital 311 Pleasant Ave. 55102	227–6521 Ext. 343	Edwin C. Burklund, M.D. Marilyn Day, R.N.
	St. John's Hospital 403 Maria Ave. 55106	228–3132	Mrs. Barbara H. Vadnais, R. Ph.
	St. Joseph's Hospital 69 W. Exchange 55102	222–2861 Ext. 348, 349	John J. Galligan, M.D.
	St. Luke's Hospital 300 Pleasant Ave. c/o Emergency Room 55102	228–8201	J. S. Henry, M.D. Dolores Wiggin, R.N.

City	Name and Address	Telephone	Director and Assistant Director
(Minnesota—Continued)			
St. Paul	Poison Information Center St. Paul–Ramsey Hospital 640 Jackson St. 55101	222–4260 Ext. 215	Robert A. Van Tyn, M.D.
Virginia	Poison Information Center Virginia Municipal Hospital 55792	741–8340	W. P. Engelstad, M.D.
Willmar	Poison Information Center Rice Memorial Hospital 56201	235–4543 Ext. 56	Robert D. Fedor, M.D. Miss Evelyn Heil
Worthington	Poison Information Center Worthington Municipal Hospital 56187	376–4141 Ext. 32 Night: 376–6834	M. W. Plucker, M.D. Warren Gordon, R. Ph.

MISSISSIPPI

City	Name and Address	Telephone	Director and Assistant Director
STATE COORDINATOR ...	State Board of Health Jackson 39205	354–6650	Durward Blakey, M.D. Director, Division of Preventable Disease Control
Brandon	Poison Control Center Rankin General Hospital 350 Grossgates Blvd. 39042	825–2811 Ext. 626	Nicholas D. House, R. Ph. Richard K. Foster, R. Ph.

Columbia	Poison Control Center Marion County General Hospital 39429	736–6303 Ext. 217	Tommie R. Pittman, R. Ph. Mrs. Jean Conerly, R.N.
Greenwood	Poison Control Center Greenwood-LeFlore Hospital River Road 38930	453–9751 Ext. 231	Joseph L. Hinton, R. Ph. Glenn A. Doty III, R. Ph.
Hattiesburg	Poison Control Information Center Forrest County General Hospital 400 S. 28th Ave. 39401	582–8361 Ext. 46	Bill W. Elkins, R. Ph. Harvey Lofton, R. Ph.
Jackson	Poison Control Center Baptist Hospital 1190 N. State St. 39201	948–5211 Ext. 201, 202, 203	Harvey F. Garrison, M.D.
	Poison Control Center St. Dominic–Jackson Memorial Hospital 969 Lakeland Dr. 39216	266–5281	Ray L. Butler, R. Ph. Jerry M. Perry, R. Ph.
	State Board of Health Division of Preventable Disease Control 39205	354–6650	Durward Blakey, M.D.
Keesler Air Force Base (Biloxi)	Poison Control Center USAF Hospital Keesler Keesler Air Force Base 39534	432–1521 Ext. 284	Fred R. Stowe, M.D.
Laurel	Poison Control Center Jones County Community Hospital Jefferson St. at 13th Ave. 39440	425–1441 Ext. 20, 48	Joel H. McKinley, R. Ph. Robert C. Boyd, R. Ph.

City	Name and Address	Telephone	Director and Assistant Director
(Mississippi—Continued)			
Meridian	Poison Control Center St. Joseph Hospital Highway 39, N. 39301	483–6211 Ext. 54, 42	Ronald Stephenson, R. Ph. Emmett Berry, Jr., R. Ph.
Pascagoula	Poison Control Center Singing River Hospital Highway 90E 39567	762–6121 Ext. 761	Mrs. Sara F. Fornea, R. Ph.
University	Poison Control Center School of Pharmacy University of Mississippi 38677	234–1522	Joe B. McCaskill Mrs. Sandra A. Smith
Vicksburg	Poison Control Center Mercy Hospital–Street Memorial 100 McAuley Dr. 39181	636–2121 Ext. 302, 255, 256	S. K. Love, M.D. Mrs. Doris Cassidy, R. Ph.

MISSOURI

City	Name and Address	Telephone	Director and Assistant Director
STATE COORDINATOR ...	Missouri Division of Health Jefferson City 65101	635–4111	Stephen B. Jones, Director Accident Prevention Program
Cape Girardeau	Poison Control Center St. Francis Hospital 825 Good Hope St. 63701	334–4461 Ext. 49	G. R. Weeks, M.D. James O. Alyea, M.D.

Columbia	Poison Control Center University of Missouri Medical Center 807 Stadium Blvd. 65201	442–5111	Clement E. Brooke, M.D.
Hannibal	Poison Control Center St. Elizabeth Hospital 109 Virginia St. 63401	221–0414 Ext. 213	J. H. Waltersheid, M.D. Fred Tonnies, R.N.
Joplin	Poison Control Center St. John's Hospital 2727 McClelland Blvd. 64801	781–2727 Ext. 276	N. H. Barnett, M.D. Joe P. Brasel, R. Ph.
Kansas City	Poison Control Center Children's Mercy Hospital 24th & Gillham Rd. 64108	471–0626 Ext. 220	Ned W. Smull, M.D. George W. Wise, M.D.
	Poison Control Center Kansas City General Hospital and Medical Center 23rd & Cherry St. 64108	HA 1–8060 Ext. 257, 235	W. K. McNabney, M.D. Jean Armstrong, R.N.
Kirksville	Poison Control Center Kirksville Osteopathic Hospital 800 W. Jefferson St. 63501	665–4611 Ext. 240	Richard H. Mercer, D.O. Martin Lowry, D.O.
Poplar Bluff	Poison Control Center Lucy Lee Hospital 330 N. 2nd Street 63901	785–7721 Ext. 33	Charles A. Raper, M.D. B. M. McLain, M.D.
Rolla	Poison Control Center Phelps County Memorial Hospital 1000 W. 10th St. 65401	364–3100 Ext. 31	Barbara E. Russell, M.D. Robert B. Young, M.D.

City	Name and Address	Telephone	Director and Assistant Director
(Missouri—Continued)			
St. Joseph	Poison Control Center Methodist Hospital and Medical Center 8th & Faraon Sts. 64501	232–8461 Ext. 277	H. E. Petersen, M.D. H. C. Senne, M.D. Martin Christ, M.D.
St. Louis	Poison Control Center Cardinal Glennon Children's Memorial Hospital 1465 S. Grand Ave. 63104	865–4000 Ext. 417	Fernando de Castro, M.D. Ursula Rolfe, M.D.
	Poison Control Center St. Louis Children's Hospital 500 S. Kingshighway 63110	367–6880 Ext. 220	J. Neal Middelkamp, M.D. Dorothy J. Jones, M.D.
Springfield	Poison Control Center Lester E. Cox Medical Center 1423 N. Jefferson St. 65802	865–9631 Ext. 253, 254	Paul S. Quinn, M.D. Noel R. Lewis, M.D.
	Poison Control Center St. John's Hospital 1235 E. Cherokee 65804	881–8811 Ext. 248, 241	Michael J. Clarke, M.D. Richard Loeb, M.D.
West Plains	Poison Control Center West Plains Memorial Hospital 1103 Alaska Ave. 65775	256–8141 Ext. 8	Marvin L. Fowler, M.D. Charlotte Van Bibber, R.N.

MONTANA

STATE COORDINATOR	State Department of Health Helena 59601	449-2544	John S. Anderson, M.D. Executive Officer and Secretary
Bozeman	Poison Control Center Bozeman Deaconess Hospital 15 West Lamme 59715	586-5431	Loxenia M. Wald, R.N.
Helena	Poison Control Center St. Peter's Hospital 59601	442-2480 Ext. 317	Donald E. Espelin, M.D. Denis R. Yost, R. Ph.

NEBRASKA

STATE COORDINATOR	State Department of Health Lincoln 68509	477-5211	H. E. McConnell, Dr. Director, Division of Laboratories
Lincoln	Poison Control Center Bryan Memorial Hospital 4848 Sumner St. 68506	473-3244	Oliver V. Waite, DDS Mel J. Epp, M.D.
Omaha	Poison Control Center Children's Memorial Hospital 44th & Dewey Sts. 68105	558-5400 Poison Control	Theodore Pfundt, M.D. Anthony Lombardo, M.D.

NEVADA

STATE COORDINATOR	Department of Health & Welfare Carson City 89701	882-7458	Chief, Bureau of Preventive Medicine

City	Name and Address	Telephone	Director and Assistant Director
(Nevada—Continued)			
Las Vegas	Poison Control Center Southern Nevada Memorial Hospital 1800 West Charleston Blvd. 89102	385-1277	Robert R. Belliveau, M.D.
Reno	Poison Control Center Washoe Medical Center Kirman & Mills Sts. 89502	785-4129	V. A. Salvadorini, M.D. James W. Decker, M.D.

NEW HAMPSHIRE

City	Name and Address	Telephone	Director and Assistant Director
STATE COORDINATOR ...	Department of Health & Welfare Concord 03301	225-6611	Ursula Sanders, M.D. Director, Division of Maternal & Child Health & Crippled Children's Services
Hanover	Poison Information Center Mary Hitchcock Hospital 2 Maynard St. 03755	643-4000	Robert E. Gosselin, M.D.

NEW JERSEY

STATE COORDINATOR	State Department of Health Trenton 08625	292–5616	Edmond Duffy, Jr.
Atlantic City	Poison Control Center Atlantic City Hospital 1925 Pacific Ave. 08401	344–4081 Ext. 228	Morton Leach, M.D. Mrs. Vera Davies, R.N.
Belleville	Poison Control Center Clara Maass Hospital 1A Franklin Ave. 07109	751–1000 Ext. 781	Robert Lorello, M.D.
Boonton	Poison Control Center Riverside Hospital Powerville Rd. 07005	334–5000 Ext. 55	Dr. Friedensohn Mrs. Anne Mack, R.N.
Bridgeton	Poison Control Center Bridgeton Hospital Irving Ave. 08302	451–6600	James G. Iannucci, M.D. Rose Cooker, R.N.
Camden	Poison Control Center West Jersey Hospital Mt. Ephraim & Atlantic Aves. 08104	963–8830 Ext. 351	James Spiro, M.D. Michael Sarik, M.D.
Denville	Poison Control Center St. Clare's Hospital Pocono Rd. 07834	627–3000 Ext. 208	Perry Zevin, M.D.
East Orange	Poison Control Center East Orange General Hospital 300 Central Ave. 07019	672–8400 Ext. 223	F. Fader, M.D. Mrs. B. Locascio, R.N.

City	Name and Address	Telephone	Director and Assistant Director
(New Jersey—Continued)			
Elizabeth	Poison Control Center St. Elizabeth Hospital 225 Williamson St. 07207	289-4000 Ext. 351	Robert Wegryn, M.D.
Englewood	Poison Control Center Englewood Hospital 350 Engle Ave. 07631	568-3400 Ext. 391	John Shults, M.D. Eleanor Egan, R.N.
Flemington	Poison Control Center Hunterdon Medical Center Route 31 08822	782-2121	Avrum Katcher, M.D.
Hasbrouck Heights	Poison Control Center Hasbrouck Heights Hospital 214 Terrace Ave. 07604	288-0800	
Livingston	Poison Control Center St. Barnabas Medical Center Old Short Hills Rd. 07039	992-5500 Ext. 467	Nathan Zukerberg, M.D.
Long Branch	Poison Control Center Monmouth Medical Center 255 2nd Ave. 07740	222-2210	Murray Kessler, M.D.

Montclair	Poison Control Center Mountainside Hospital Bay & Highland Aves. 07042	746-6000 Ext. 234	Harold Mancusi-Ungaro M.D. Fred Douglas, M.D.
Morristown	Poison Control Center All Souls Hospital 95 Mount Kemble Ave. 07960	538-0900 Ext. 220	S. Giordano, M.D. A. Wrege, R.N.
Mount Holly	Poison Control Center Burlington County Memorial Hospital 175 Madison Ave. 08060	267-0700 Ext. 255	Graham P. Jones, M.D. Joan Fitzgerald
Neptune	Poison Control Center Jersey Shore Medical Center-Fitkin 1945 Corlies Ave. 07753	988-1818	Michael Quatrella, M.D. Mrs. Costello
Newark	Poison Control Center Children's Hospital of Newark United Hospitals 15 S. 9th St. 07107	484-8000 Ext. 419	Carl Ross, M.D.
	Poison Control Center Newark Beth Israel Hospital 201 Lyons Ave. 07112	923-6000	Dr. Parent
New Brunswick	Poison Control Center Middlesex General Hospital 180 Somerset St. 08901	828-3000	William Kuhn, M.D. Flora Sarra, R.N.
	Poison Control Center St. Peter's General Hospital Easton. Ave. 08903	545-8000 Ext. 329	Dr. Winn

City	Name and Address	Telephone	Director and Assistant Director
(New Jersey—Continued)			
Newton	Poison Control Center Newton Memorial Hospital 175 High St. 07860	383-2121 Ext. 226	Robert A. Weinstein, M.D.
Orange	Poison Control Center Hospital Center at Orange 188 S. Essex Ave. 07051	678-1100 Ext. 231	Robert Jennings, M.D.
Passaic	Poison Control Center St. Mary's Hospital 211 Pennington Ave. 07055	473-1000 Ext. 341	Alfredo Cruz, M.D.
Paterson	Poison Control Center Paterson General Hospital 528 Market St. 07501	684-6900 Ext. 330	Alfred A. Siss, M.D. Fred A. Botting
Perth Amboy	Poison Control Center Perth Amboy General Hospital 530 New Brunswick Ave. 08861	442-3700 Ext. 374	E. McGinley, M.D.
Phillipsburg	Poison Control Center Warren Hospital 185 Roseberry St. 08865	859-1500 Ext. 278	E. Barbara Lorentz, M.D.

Point Pleasant	Poison Control Center Point Pleasant Hospital Osborn Ave. & River Front 08743	892–1100 Ext. 266	Arnold S. Lane
Princeton	Poison Control Center Princeton Hospital 253 Witherspoon St. 08540	921–7700 Ext. 241	Thomas P. Cortelyou, M.D.
Saddle Brook	Poison Control Center Saddle Brook Hospital 300 Market St. 07662	843–6700	John C. Pellosie, M.D. Margaret Anderson, R.N.
Somers Point	Poison Control Center Shore Memorial Hospital New York & Sunny Aves. 08244	927–3501 Ext. 208	Mae Brassil, R.N.
Somerville	Poison Control Center Somerset Hospital Rehill Ave. 08876	725–4000 Ext. 203	M. Tolomeo, M.D.
Summit	Poison Control Center Overlook Hospital 193 Morris Ave. 07901	273–8100 Ext. 417	Dr. Coppola Mrs. Jean Green, R.N.
Teaneck	Poison Control Center Holy Name Hospital 718 Teaneck Rd. 07666	837–3070 Ext. 355	J. S. Meehan, M.D. Mrs. M. Loveman, R.N.
Trenton	Poison Control Center Helene Fuld Hospital 750 Brunswick Ave. 08638	396–6575 Ext. 378	Irving W. Robinson, M.D. Thomas Hayes, R. Ph.

City	Name and Address	Telephone	Director and Assistant Director
(New Jersey—Continued)			
Union	Poison Control Center Memorial General Hospital 100 Galloping Hill Rd. 07083	687–1900 Ext. 238	M. Belkoff, M.D.

NEW MEXICO

City	Name and Address	Telephone	Director and Assistant Director
STATE COORDINATOR ...	Department of Public Health Santa Fe 87501	827–2663	Don F. Thompson Food Protection Unit, Health and Social Services, Environmental Services Division
Alamogordo	Poison Control Center Gerald Champion Memorial Hospital 1209 9th St. 88310	437–3770 Ext. 260	William E. LaBarre, M.D.
Albuquerque	Poison Control Center Bernalillo County Indian Hospital 2211 Lomas Blvd., N.E. 87106	265–4411	Frances Blair, R. Ph.

Carlsbad	Poison Control Center Carlsbad Regional Medical Center Northgate Unit, Box 1479 88220	887–3521 Ext. 266	John A. Most, M.D.
Clovis	Poison Control Center Clovis Memorial Hospital Box 231, 1210 Thornton Street 88101	763–4493 Ext. 131	H. McClintock, M.D.
Las Cruces	Poison Control Center Memorial General Hospital Alameda & Lohman 88001	524–8641 Ext. 25, 61	J. S. Drake, M.D.
Ratón	Poison Control Center Miners' Hospital of New Mexico S. 6th St. 87740	445–2741 Ext. 26	Milton Floersheim, Jr., M.D. June Brooks, R.N.
Roswell	Poison Control Center Eastern New Mexico Medical Center 405 Country Club Rd. 88201	622–8170 Ext. 26	K. L. Bergener, M.D. J. Ronald Ewing, R. Ph.

NEW YORK

| STATE COORDINATOR | State Department of Health
Albany 12208 | RG 4–2121 | Selig Katz, M.D., Bureau of Maternal and Child Health |
| Albany | Poison Control Center
Albany Medical Center
New Scotland Ave. 12208 | 462–7521 | Paul R. Patterson, M.D. |

City	Name and Address	Telephone	Director and Assistant Director
(New York—Continued)			
Binghamton	Poison Control Center Binghamton General Hospital Mitchell Ave. 13903	772–1100 Ext. 431	Patrick E. O'Hara, M.D. Edward Gilmore, M.D.
	Poison Control Center Our Lady of Lourdes Memorial Hospital 169 Riverside Dr. 13904	729–6521	Richard E. Sullivan, M.D. Lucille Romano, R.N.
Buffalo	Poison Control Center Buffalo Children's Hospital 219 Bryant St. 14222	878–7374 878–7503	Sumner J. Yaffe, M.D. Basil Continelli, R. Ph.
Dunkirk	Poison Control Center Brooks Memorial Hospital 10 W. 6th St. 14048	366–1111 Ext. 414, 415	Arnold B. Victor, M.D. Phyliss Andrews, R.N.
East Meadow	Poison Control Center Meadowbrook Hospital P.O. Box 175 11554	542–2323 542–2324	Howard C. Mofenson, M.D. Joseph Greensher, M.D.
Elmira	Poison Control Center Arnot Ogden Memorial Hospital Roe Ave. & Grove St. 14901	734–5221 Ext. 237, 238, 331	John Forrest, M.D.

	Poison Control Center St. Joseph's Hospital 555 E. Market St. 14901	733–6541 Ext. 213, 271	Robert A. Sofia, R. Ph.
Endicott	Poison Control Center Ideal Hospital of Endicott 600 High Ave. 13760	754–7171 Ext. 66	Lawrence M. Gibbs, R. Ph.
Ithaca	Poison Control Center Tompkins County Hospital 1285 Trumansburg Rd. 14850	272–7480 Ext. 275, 283	E. G. Arnold A. D. Broadhead, R. Ph.
Jamestown	Poison Control Center Jamestown General Hospital Hospital Park 14701	484–1161 Ext. 52	Harriett E. Northrup, M.D.
	Poison Control Center W. C. A. Hospital 207 Foote Ave. 14701	487–0141	Harriett E. Northrup, M.D. Mildred Withington, R.N.
Johnson City	Poison Control Center Wilson Memorial Hospital 33–57 Harrison St. 13790	797–1211 Ext. 268	Joseph F. Martinak, M.D. Jack Detrick, R. Ph.
Kingston	Poison Control Center Kingston Hospital 396 Broadway 12401	331–3131 Ext. 250	William E. Askue, M.D.
New York	Poison Control Center New York City Department of Health 455 1st Ave. 10016	340–4494	Harry W. Raybin

City	Name and Address	Telephone	Director and Assistant Director
(New York—Continued)			
Niagara Falls	Poison Control Center Niagara Falls Memorial Hospital 621 10th St. 14302	285-2571 Ext. 253	Maria Crea, M.D.
Nyack	Poison Control Center Nyack Hospital N. Midland Ave. 10960	EL 8-6200 Ext. 223	Irwin Danziger, M.D.
Oswego	Poison Control Center Oswego Hospital 110 W. 6th St. 13126	FI 3-1920	John S. Puzauskas, M.D.
Rochester	Poison Control Center University of Rochester Medical Center and Strong Memorial Hospital 260 Crittenden Blvd. 14620	275-3232	Ruth A. Lawrence, M.D.
Syracuse	Poison Control Center Upstate Medical Center 750 E. Adams St. 13210	GR 6-3166	Virginia G. Harris, M.D. Howard Weinberger, M.D.

Warsaw	Poison Control Center Wyoming County Community Hospital 400 N. Main St. 14569	796–2233	P. Burgeson, M.D. C. Butler, R.N.
Watertown	Poison Information Center House of the Good Samaritan Hospital Washington & Pratt Sts. 13602	782–8110	B. J. Ebbels, M.D. R. J. Marilley, M.D.

NORTH CAROLINA

STATE COORDINATOR ...	State Board of Health Raleigh 27602	829–3446	Miss Nettie F. Day, Chief Accident Prevention Section, Division of Epidemiology
Asheville	Poison Control Center Memorial Mission Hospital 509 Biltmore Ave. 28807	252–5331 Ext. 262	Mary H. McConnell, M.D.
Charlotte	Poison Control Center Mercy Hospital 2000 E. 5th St. 28204	334–6831	Gilbert D. Colina T. Lucas, Jr., M.D.
Durham	Poison Control Center Duke University Hospital Box 3024 27706	684–8111 Ext. 3957	Jay M. Arena, M.D. Shirley K. Osterhout, M.D.
Hendersonville	Poison Control Center Margaret R. Pardee Hospital Fleming St. 28739	693–6522 Ext. 242	Fletcher L. Raiford, M.D. Margaret Gretz, R. Ph.

City	Name and Address	Telephone	Director and Assistant Director
(North Carolina—Continued)			
Jacksonville	Poison Control Center Onslow Memorial Hospital College St. 28540	347-1241	S. C. Cox, M.D. Eleanor Williams, M.D.
Wilmington	Poison Control Center New Hanover Memorial Hospital 2431 S. 17th St. 28401	763-9021 Ext. 311, 312	Charles Hicks, M.D. M. E. Underwood, R. Ph.

NORTH DAKOTA

City	Name and Address	Telephone	Director and Assistant Director
STATE COORDINATOR	State Department of Health Bismarck 58501	224-2348	Injury Control Program
Bismarck	Poison Control Center Quain and Ranstad Clinic Burleigh County 58501	223-1420 Night: 223-5000 Night: 223-4700	R. B. Tudor, M.D. H. P. Smeenk, M.D.
Dickinson	Poison Control Center St. Joseph's Hospital 7th St. W. 58601	225-6771 Ext. 329, 259	Jerome J. Wahl, R. Ph. Sister Virginia

Fargo .... Poison Control Center
North Dakota State University
Pharmacology Department 58102 — 237-8115 — Stephen M. Sleight, R. Ph.
Mike R. Sather, R. Ph.

Grand Forks .... Poison Control Center
Grand Forks Deaconess Hospital
212 S. 4th St.
P.O. Box 1718 58201 — 775-4241 — Jerome Dufault, R. Ph.

Jamestown .... Poison Control Center
Jamestown Hospital
419 5th St. N.E. 58401 — 252-1050 — John A. Beall, M.D.
Edwin O. Hieb, M.D.

Minot .... Poison Control Center
St. Joseph's Hospital
304 4th St. 58701 — 838-0341 Ext. 253 — Gale Richardson, M.D.
Richard Brey, R. Ph.

Williston .... Poison Control Center
Mercy Hospital
Washington Avenue & Broadway
58801 — 572-2188 — G. E. Ellis, M.D.

OHIO

STATE
COORDINATOR ... Department of Health
Columbus 43216 — 469-2544 — Tom Magoto, Sanitarian in Charge, Accident Prevention Unit

Akron .... Poison Control Center
Children's Hospital
182 Bowery St. 44308 — 253-5531 Ext. 246 — Max Griffin, M.D.

City	Name and Address	Telephone	Director and Assistant Director
(Ohio—Continued)			
Canton	Poison Information Center Aultman Hospital 2600 6th Street, S.W. 44710	452–9911 Ext. 203 454–5222	Cyril V. Gross, M.D. Richard G. Spitzer, M.D.
Cincinnati	Poison Control Center The Children's Hospital Elland & Bethesda Aves. 45229	281–6161	Robert Reece, M.D.
Cleveland	Poison Control Center Cleveland Academy of Medicine 10525 Carnegie Avenue 44106	231–3500 231–4455	Irving Sunshine, Ph. D.
Columbus	Poison Control Center The Children's Hospital 17th Street at Livingston Park 43205	258–9783	John P. Shultz, M.D.
Dayton	Poison Control Center U.S. Air Force Hospital Wright-Patterson Air Force Base 45433	257–2968	Thomas Sorauf, M.D. Ralph J. Bryan, R. Ph.
Mansfield	Poison Control Center Mansfield General Hospital 335 Glessner Ave. 44903	522–3411	James Barton, R. Ph. Dave Lautsbaugh, R. Ph.

Springfield .... Poison Control Center
The Community Hospital of Springfield & Clark County
2615 East High Street 45501
323-5531
Philip McClelland, R. Ph.
T. J. Williams, M.D.

Toledo .... Poison Information Center
Maumee Valley Hospital
2025 Arlington Ave. 43609
382-3435
Marian Rejent, M.D.
Robert Fulton, R. Ph.

Youngstown .... Poison Control Center
St. Elizabeth Hospital
1044 Belmont Ave. 44505
746-7231 Ext. 200, 201, 204
Kurt J. Wegner, M.D.
Sr. M. Michael

OKLAHOMA

STATE COORDINATOR ... State Department of Health
Oklahoma City 73111
427-6232
F. R. Hassler, M.D., Chief, Laboratory Services and Communicable Disease Control

Lawton .... Poison Control Center
Comanche County Memorial Hospital
Gore Blvd. 73501
355-8620 Ext. 232, 234
Marjorie Roberts, R.N.
DeWayne Younger, R.N.

Oklahoma City ..... Poison Control Center
State Department of Health
Laboratory Services and Communicable Disease Control
3400 N. Eastern 73111
427-6232
F. R. Hassler, M.D.
H. E. Maxey

City	Name and Address	Telephone	Director and Assistant Director
(Oklahoma—Continued)			
Ponca City	Poison Control Center Ponca City Hospital 14th & Virginia Ave. 74601	765-3321 Ext. 372	Sister Mary Ruth Keith Calvert
Tulsa	Poison Control Center Hillcrest Medical Center 1120 S. Utica Ave. 74104	584-1351 Ext. 598	Leo Lowbeer, M.D.

OREGON

City	Name and Address	Telephone	Director and Assistant Director
Portland	Poison Control Registry Pediatrics Department University of Oregon Medical School 3181 S.W. Sam Jackson Park Rd. 97201	228-9181 Ext. 370 Night-Emergency Room	Emily Tufts, M.D.

PENNSYLVANIA

City	Name and Address	Telephone	Director and Assistant Director
STATE COORDINATOR ...	State Department of Health Harrisburg 17120	787-6436	P. W. Wilcox, Drug Program Consultant, Division of Drug Control

Allentown	Poison Control Center Allentown Hospital Association 17th & Chew Sts. 18102	434-7161 Ext. 226	Headley S. White, Jr., M.D.
Chambersburg	Poison Control Center The Chambersburg Hospital 7th & King Sts. 17201	264-5171	Owen Hartman, M.D.
Chester	Poison Control Center Sacred Heart General Hospital 9th & Wilson Sts. 19013	494-0721	Joseph Feingold, M.D. Zbigneu Grabowski, R. Ph.
Danville	Poison Control Center George F. Giesinger Memorial Hospital Montour County 17821	275-1000 Ext. 591	Michael L. Daly, Jr, M.D.
Easton	Poison Control Center Easton Hospital 21st & Lehigh Sts. 18042	258-6221 Ext. 235, 210, 321	Agatha Costanza, M.D.
East Stroudsburg	Poison Control Center General Hospital of Monroe County 206 E. Brown St. 18301	421-4000 Ext. 740	Edward T. Horn, Jr., M.D. Janet Conrader, R.N.
Erie	Poison Control Center Erie Osteopathic Hospital 5515 Peach St. 16509	864-4031 Ext. 27	Owen W. Short, M.D. Lois M. Jedynski, R.N.
	Poison Control Center Hamot Hospital Association Second & State Sts. 16512	455-6711 Ext. 521	William Loose, M.D. A. J. Baloga, R.N.

City	Name and Address	Telephone	Director and Assistant Director
(Pennsylvania—Continued)			
Erie	Poison Control Center St. Vincent Hospital 232 W. 25th St. 16512	453-6911 Ext. 216, 345	Daniel S. Snow, M.D. Sister Marie Paul, R.N.
Hanover	Poison Control Center Hanover General Hospital 300 Highland Ave. 17331	637-3711 Ext. 111	Gabriel Zelesnick, M.D. Donald Withers, M.D.
Harrisburg	Poison Control Center Harrisburg Hospital Front & Mulberry Sts. 17101	782-3639	Rosemarie J. Tursky, M.D.
	Poison Control Center Polyclinic Hospital 3rd and Polyclinic Ave. 17105	782-4141 Ext. 4132	Euryryn Jones, M.D. Jane Fields, R.N.
Johnstown	Poison Control Center Mercy Hospital 1020 Franklin St. 15905	535-5353	David C. Borecky, M.D. Dorothy Behe, R.N.
Lancaster	Poison Control Center St. Joseph's Hospital 250 College Ave. 17604	397-2821 Ext. 201	D. B. Coursin, M.D. Sr. Ann Charles

Latrobe	Poison Control Center Latrobe Area Hospital Association 2nd Ave. 15650	539-9711	Walter W. Jetter, M.D. Jack Kay, R. Ph.
Lewistown	Poison Control Center Lewistown Hospital Highland Ave. 17044	248-5411 Ext. 247	Charles L. Eater, Jr., M.D. Donald E. Basom, M.D.
Philadelphia	Poison Information Center Department of Public Health University Avenue & Curie St. 19104	WA 2-5523	Jane H. Speaker, Ph. D.
Pittsburgh	Poison Control Center Children's Hospital 125 Desoto St. 15213	681-6669	G. A. Friday, M.D. E. W. Saitz, M.D.
	Poison Control Center St. John's General Hospital 3339 McClure Ave. 15212	766-8300	Henry E. West, R. Ph. W. C. McCarthy, M. D.
Scranton	Poison Control Center Community Medical Center 316 Colfax Ave. 18510	343-5566	Marion Williams, R.N.
Sharon	Poison Control Center Sharon General Hospital 740 E. State St. 16146	981-1700 Ext. 281	Theodore Yarboro, M.D. Hilbert Beloff, R. Ph.
Wilkes-Barre	Poison Control Center The Mercy Hospital of Wilkes-Barre 196 Hanover St. 18703	822-8101 Ext. 274, 305, 306	Joseph Robinson, M.D.

City	Name and Address	Telephone	Director and Assistant Director
(Pennsylvania—Continued)			
Wilkes-Barre	Poison Control Center Wilkes-Barre General Hospital North River & Auburn Streets 18702	823–1121 Ext. 222	
York	Poison Control Center Memorial Osteopathic Hospital 325 S. Belmont St. 17403	843–8623 Ext. 274, 275	James M. Hotham, M.D. Mr. Mummert, R. Ph.
	Poison Control Center York Hospital George Street & Rathton Road 17403	854–1511	Furman T. Updyke, M.D. E. Wilson Nollau, R. Ph.

PUERTO RICO

City	Name and Address	Telephone	Director and Assistant Director
STATE COORDINATOR ...	University of Puerto Rico Rio Piedras	765–4880 765–0615	Sidney Kaye, Ph. D.
Aguadilla	Poison Control Center District Hospital of Aguadilla 00603	891–0200	Pedro Mendoza, M.D.
Arecibo	Poison Control Center District Hospital of Arecibo 00613	878–3535	

Fajardo .... Poison Control Center   863-0505   Rafael Franco Santiago, M.D.
                     District Hospital of Fajardo 00649

Mayaguez .... Poison Control Center   832-8686   Ismael Rodriguez Ibanez, M.D.
                     Mayaguez Medical Center
                     Department of Health
                     P.O. Box 1868 00709

Ponce .... Poison Control Center   842-8964   Luis A. Rosario, M.D.
                     District Hospital of Ponce 00731   842-2080

San Juan .... Poison Control Center   764-3515
                     Medical Center of Puerto Rico

RHODE ISLAND

STATE
COORDINATOR ... State Department of Health   521-7100   George A. Kenny
                  Providence 02903   Chief, Division of Public
                                                                                    Health, Education and
                                                                                    Research

Kingston .... Poison Control Center   792-2763   Heber W. Youngken, Jr., Ph. D.
                     College of Pharmacy   John J. DeFeo, Ph. D.
                     University of Rhode Island 02881

Pawtucket .... Poison Control Center   724-1230   Harold Woodcome, M.D.
                     Memorial Hospital   Joseph E. Foley, R.N.
                     Prospect St. 02860

Providence .... Poison Control Center   277-4000   Joseph S. Karas, M.D.
                     Rhode Island Hospital
                     593 Eddy St. 02902

City	Name and Address	Telephone	Director and Assistant Director
(Rhode Island—Continued)			
Providence	Poison Control Center Roger Williams General Hospital 825 Chalkstone Ave. 02908	521–5055 Ext. 461	Robert H. Durie, M.D. Shirley D'Ambra, R.N.

SOUTH CAROLINA

City	Name and Address	Telephone	Director and Assistant Director
STATE COORDINATOR ...	State Board of Health Columbia 29201	758–5664	Hilla Sheriff, M.D., Chief, Bureau Community Health Services
Charleston	Poison Control Center Medical College Hospital 80 Barre St. 29401	792–0211 (Ask to page control center)	Margaret Q. Jenkins, M.D.
Columbia	Poison Control Center Columbia Hospital 2020 Hampton St. 29204	254–7382	Benjamin O. Stands, M.D.

SOUTH DAKOTA

STATE
COORDINATOR ...State Department of Health   224-5911   G. J. Van Heuvelen, M.D.
                Pierre 57501   State Health Officer

Sioux Falls ....Poison Control Center   336-3894   G. F. Tuohy, M.D.
                McKennan Hospital   Ron Huether, R. Ph.
                800 East 21st St. 57101

Vermillion ....Poison Control Center   624-3432   J. N. Spencer, Ph. D.
                University of South Dakota   K. L. Bailey, Ph. D.
                Department of Pharmacology 57069

TENNESSEE

STATE
COORDINATOR ...State Department of Public Health   741-3644   William H. Armes, Jr., M.D.
                Nashville 37219   Division of Preventive Health
                                                                Services

Chattanooga ....Poison Control Center   624-5020   Ronald Eith, M.D.
                T.C. Thompson Children's   Mrs. Marilyn Mann, R.N.
                Hospital
                1001 Glenwood Dr. 37406

Columbia ....Poison Control Center   388-2320   Kenneth A. Flowers, R. Ph.
                Maury County Hospital   Ext. 49
                Mt. Pleasant Pike 38401

Jackson ....Poison Control Center   424-0424   Chester K. Jones, M.D.
                Madison General Hospital   Ext. 241
                708 W. Forest 38301

City	Name and Address	Telephone	Director and Assistant Director
(Tennessee—Continued)			
Johnson City	Poison Control Center Memorial Hospital Boone & Fairview Ave. 37601	926-1131 Ext. 330	J. R. Bowman, M.D.
Knoxville	Poison Control Center University of Tennessee Memorial Research Center Alcoa Highway 37920	971-3261	Robert F. Lash, M.D.
Memphis	Poison Control Center Le Bonheur Children's Hospital Adams Avenue at Dunlap 38103	525-6541 Ext. 281	Albert H. Price, R. Ph. O. P. Walker, R. Ph.
Nashville	Poison Control Center Vanderbilt Hospital 1161 21st Ave. S. 37203	322-2351	John Wilson, M.D. Wayne I. Hayes

TEXAS

City	Name and Address	Telephone	Director and Assistant Director
STATE COORDINATOR	State Department of Health Austin 78756	GL 3-6631	H. F. Adrian, Engineer, Industrial Hygiene Program, Division of Occupational Health

Abilene	Poison Control Center Hendrick Memorial Hospital 19th & Hickory Sts. 79601	677-1011	Herman E. Schaffer, M.D.
Amarillo	Poison Control Center Northwest Texas Hospital 2203 W. 6th St. 79106	376-4431 Ext. 321	Maurice E. Dyer, M.D.
Austin	Poison Control Center Brackenridge Hospital 14th & Sabine Sts. 78701	478-4490	K. Dyo, M.D.
Beaumont	Poison Control Center Baptist Hospital of Southeast Texas College & 11th St. Box 1591 77701	833-7409	Marvin A. Laurent, Jr., R. Ph. W. P. Robert, Jr., M.D.
Corpus Christi	Poison Control Center Memorial Hospital Medical Library 2606 Hospital Building Box 5008 78405	884-4511 Ext. 273	Meyer Kurzner, M.D. Roy G. Sandoval, R. Ph.
El Paso	Poison Control Center R.E. Thomason General Hospital 4815 Alameda Ave. 79905	544-1200	Paul Huchton, M.D. Laurance N. Nickey, M.D.
Fort Worth	Poison Control Center W.I. Cook Memorial Hospital 1212 W. Lancaster Ave. 76102	ED 6-5521 Ext. 17 Night: ED 6-5527	Edward M. Wier, M.D. Paul V. Wallace, Jr.

City	Name and Address	Telephone	Director and Assistant Director
(Texas—Continued)			
Galveston	Poison Control Center Medical Branch Hospital University of Texas 8th & Mechanic Sts. 77550	765–1420 765–2408	Joe B. Nash, Ph. D. Eustacio Galvan, R. Ph.
Grand Prairie	Poison Control Center Mid-Cities Memorial Hospital 2733 Sherman Rd. 75050	264–1651 Ext. 18	R. L. Nelson, M.D. H. Locke, M.D.
Harlingen	Poison Control Center Valley Baptist Hospital 2101 S. Commerce St. 78550	423–1224 Ext. 23	George L. Gallaher, M.D. George J. Toland, Jr., M.D.
Laredo	Poison Control Center Mercy Hospital 1515 Logan 78040	722–2431 Ext. 29	Joaquin Gonzalez Cigarroa, Jr., M.D.
Lubbock	Poison Control Center Methodist Hospital 3615 19th St. 79410	SW 2–1011 Ext. 315	Bill Woodward, R. Ph. Don Hallmark, R. Ph.
Midland	Poison Control Center Midland Memorial Hospital 1908 W. Wall 79701	682–7381 Emergency Room	John W. Foster, M.D. M. E. Waddell, R.N.

Odessa	Poison Control Center Medical Center Hospital 600 W. 4th St. 79760	337–7311 Ext. 250	William D. Furst, M.D. Edwin C. Dempsey, M.D.
Plainview	Poison Control Center Plainview Hospital 2404 Yonkers St. 79072	296–9601	Dorothy Long, M.D. Ruby Duvall
San Angelo	Poison Control Center Shannon West Texas Memorial Hospital 9 S. Magdalen St. 76901	653–6741 Ext. 210	H. M. Anderson, M.D. Dallas E. Dill, R. Ph.
San Antonio	Poison Control Center Bexar County Hospital District 7703 Floyd Curl Dr. 78229	223–1481	Alexander W. Pierce, Jr., M.D. Fernando A. Guerra, M.D.
Texarkana	Poison Control Center Wadley Hospital 1000 Pine St. 75501	793–4511	Lloyd M. Greenwell Jerry Gates, R.N.
Tyler	Poison Control Center Medical Center Hospital 1000 S. Beckham St. 75701	594–9361 Ext. 255	John Reuland, M.D. George B. Pearson
Waco	Poison Information Center Hillcrest Hospital 3000 Herring Ave. 76708	753–1412	R. E. Henderson, Jr., M.D.
Wharton	Poison Control Center Caney Valley Memorial Hospital 503 N. Resident St. 77488	523–2440 Ext. 213 Night: LE 2–1440	L. B. Outlar, M.D. C. B. Williams, R.N.

City	Name and Address	Telephone	Director and Assistant Director
(Texas—Continued)			
Wichita Falls	Poison Control Center Wichita General Hospital Emergency Room 1600 8th St. 76301	322-6771	George Slaughter, M.D.

UTAH

City	Name and Address	Telephone	Director and Assistant Director
STATE COORDINATOR ...	State Division of Health Salt Lake City 84113	328-6191	Taira Fukushima, M.D. Director, Bureau of Disease Prevention
	State Division of Health Salt Lake City 84113	328-6131	Russell Fraser, Director, Bureau of Laboratories
Salt Lake City	Poison Information Center University Hospital University of Utah Medical Center 84112	328-3711 Ext. 291	Alan K. Done, M.D.

VIRGIN ISLANDS

City	Name and Address	Telephone	Director and Assistant Director
STATE COORDINATOR ...	Department of Health St. Thomas 00801	774-1321 Ext. 275	John A. Starr, R. Ph. Drug and Narcotic Control

St. Croix .... Poison Control Center   773–1212   Andre C. Joseph, M.D.
                Charles Harwood Memorial   773–1311   Leatrice A. Percy, R. Ph.
                Hospital   Ext. 221
                Christiansted 00820

                Poison Control Center   772–0260   Paul Eller, M.D.
                Ingeborg Nesbitt Clinic   772–0212   Mrs. R. Hewitt, R.N.
                Fredericksted 00840

St. John .... Poison Control Center   776–1469   William Applegate, M.D.
                Morris F. DeCastro Clinic   Salvatore Tabacco, M.D.
                Cruz Bay 00830

St. Thomas .... Poison Control Center   774–1321   John A. Starr, R. Ph.
                Knud–Hansen Memorial Hospital   Ext. 266   Sussana M. Brin, R. Ph.
                00801

VIRGINIA

STATE
COORDINATOR ...State Department of Health   644–4111   Robert V. Blanke, Ph. D.
                Richmond 23219

Alexandria .... Poison Control Center   931–2000   James D. Mills, M.D.
                Alexandria Hospital   Ext. 555   William J. Weaver, Jr., M.D.
                709 Duke St. 22314

Arlington .... Poison Control Center   524–5900   William D. Dolan, M.D.
                Arlington Hospital   Ext. 662,
                5129 N. 16th St. 22205   751

City	Name and Address	Telephone	Director and Assistant Director
(Virginia—Continued)			
Blacksburg	Poison Control Center Montgomery County Community Hospital Route 460, S. 24060	951–1111	J. T. Showalter, M.D. G. M. Caldwell, M.D.
Charlottesville	Poison Control Center University of Virginia Hospital Box 307, Pediatric Clinic 22903	924–2231	W. G. Thurman, M.D. William I. Neikirk, M.D.
Danville	Poison Control Center Danville Memorial Hospital 142 S. Main St. 22201	793–6311 Ext. 257	James F. Burch
Falls Church	Poison Control Center Fairfax Hospital 3300 Gallows Rd. 22046	698–3111	R. Leidelmeyer, M.D.
Hampton	Poison Control Center Dixie Hospital Victoria Blvd. 23361	722–7921 Ext. 258, 259	Thomas W. Sale, M.D. Frank Freda, M.D.
Harrisonburg	Poison Control Center Rockingham Memorial Hospital 738 S. Mason St. 22801	434–4421 Ext. 225	Charles C. Powel, M.D. Robert L. Miller, R. Ph.

City	Center	Phone	Contact
Lexington	Poison Control Center Stonewall Jackson Hospital 22043	463–3131	F. A. Feddeman, M.D.
Lynchburg	Poison Control Center Lynchburg General Marshall Lodge Hospital, Inc. Tate Springs Rd. 24504	VI 6–6511 Ext. 203	Frank Daniel, M.D.
Nassawadox	Poison Control Center Northampton–Accomack Memorial Hospital 23413	442–2011	Blaine S. Daugherty, R. Ph. Elizabeth F. Shrieves, R.N.
Norfolk	Poison Control Center Office of Chief Medical Examiner 427 E. Charlotte St. 23510	625–1306 Ext. 4 627–3238	Ramon A. Morano
Petersburg	Poison Control Center Petersburg General Hospital Mt. Erin & Adams Sts. 23803	732–7220 Ext. 327, 328	
Portsmouth	Poison Control Center U.S. Naval Hospital 23708	397–6581 Ext. 425, 426, 427	James Hughes, M.D. Joseph Boudreaux, R. Ph.
Richmond	Poison Information Center Medical College of Virginia 1200 E. Broad St. 23219	770–5123	Robert Blanke, Ph. D. Earl Gadol, M.D.
Roanoke	Poison Control Center Roanoke Memorial Hospital Belleview & Lake Aves. 24014	342–4541 Ext. 229, 228	Andrew D. Shapiro, M.D. William H. Flannigan

City	Name and Address	Telephone	Director and Assistant Director
(Virginia—Continued)			
Staunton	Poison Control Center King's Daughters' Hospital 1410 N. Augusta St. 24401	885–0361 Ext. 247, 289	Gerald L. Selph, R. Ph. John F. Knapp, R. Ph.
Waynesboro	Poison Control Center Waynesboro Community Hospital 501 Oak Ave. 22980	942–8355 Ext. 436, 440	William C. Kappes, M.D. R. David Anderson, R. Ph.
Williamsburg	Poison Control Center Williamsburg Community Hospital Mt. Vernon Ave., Drawer H 23185	229–1120 Ext. 65	John S. Fletcher, M.D.

WASHINGTON

City	Name and Address	Telephone	Director and Assistant Director
STATE COORDINATOR ...	State Department of Health Olympia 98502	753–5871	Jess Spielholz, M.D. Acting Head, Maternal and Child Health Section
Aberdeen	Poison Control Center St. Joseph's Hospital 1006 North H St. 98520	533–0450 Ext. 42	Robert Fulton, M.D.

Olympia .... Poison Control Center
St. Peter Hospital
420 S. Sherman St. 98502

352-0301 Charles D. Kitterman, R. Ph.
P. R. Vandeman, M.D.

Pasco .... Poison Control Center
Our Lady of Lourdes Hospital
520 N. 4th Ave. 99301

547-7704 M. Magula, R.N.

Seattle .... Poison Control Center
Children's Orthopedic Hospital
4800 Sandpoint Way, N.E. 98105

LA 4-4341 William O. Robertson, M.D.
Donald A. Sutherland, M.D.

Spokane .... Poison Information Center
Deaconess Hospital
800 W. 5th Ave. 99210

RI 7-4811 Harry H. Olsen, M.D.
Anna Mae Ericksen, R.N.

Tacoma .... Poison Information Center
Mary Bridge Children's Hospital
311 S. L St. 98405

BR 2-1281
Ext. 59

Suzanne Seyler, R.N.
Lillian Hamlin, R.N.

Vancouver .... Poison Control Center
St. Joseph Community Hospital
500 E. 12th St. 98660

695-4461
Ext. 30

Barbara E. Luckman, R.N.
C. Bodin, R.N.

WEST VIRGINIA

STATE
COORDINATOR ... State Department of Health
Charleston 25305

348-2971 Eugene J. Powell,
Administrative Assistant

Beckley .... Poison Control Center
Beckley Hospital
1007 S. Oakwood Ave. 25801

252-6431
Ext. 55

Surdech Kongkasuwan, M.D.

City	Name and Address	Telephone	Director and Assistant Director
(West Virginia—Continued)			
Belle	Poison Control Center E. I. DuPont de Nemours & Co. 25015	949-4313 Ext. 261	James H. Thornbury, M.D. C. D. Gettliffe, M.D.
Charleston	Poison Control Center Charleston General Hospital Elmwood Ave. & Brook Street 25301	348-6286 Ext. 333 Night: 334	Irvin Van Meter, R. Ph.
	Poison Control Center Memorial Hospital 3200 Noyes Ave., S.E. 25304	348-4211	Darrell Richmond, R. Ph.
Clarksburg	Poison Control Center St. Mary's Hospital Washington & Chestnut Streets 26301	623-3444 Ext. 251	Samuel J. Eblen Miss Karen Paugh, R.N.
Huntington	Poison Control Center Cabell–Huntington Hospital 1340 16th St. 25701	696-6160 696-6161	William J. Kopp, M.D.
	Poison Control Center St. Mary's Hospital 2900 1st Ave. 25701	696-3762	Jack Leckie, M.D.

Martinsburg	Poison Control Center Kings Daughters Hospital 25401	267–8981 Ext. 201	William L. Rodgers, M.D. Ruth Painter, R.N.
Morgantown	Poison Control Center West Virginia University Hospital 26506	293–4451 Night: 293–5341	William G. Klingberg, M.D. Barbara Jones, M.D.
Parkersburg	Poison Control Center Camden–Clark Hospital 717 Ann St. 26101	428–8011 Ext. 28, 131	Betty Blackburn, R.N. Virginia Berry, R.N.
	Poison Control Center St. Joseph's Hospital 19th St. & Murdoch Ave. 26101	422–8535 Ext. 251	Donald R. Lantz, M.D. Peggy Heater, R.N.
Ronceverte	Poison Control Center Greenbrier Valley Hospital 608 Greenbrier Ave. 24970	647–4411 647–4412 647–4413	Ernest T. Cobb, M.D. S. Elwood Bare, R. Ph.
Weirton	Poison Control Center Weirton General Hospital St. John Road 26062	748–3232 Ext. 208	R. E. Flood, M.D.
Weston	Poison Control Center Stonewall Jackson Hospital 504 Main 26452	269–3000	Lois C. Perkins, R.N.
Wheeling	Poison Control Center Wheeling Hospital 109 Main St. 26003	233–4455 Ext. 224, 203	George E. Strobel, M.D. Suzanne Paul, R.N.

WISCONSIN

City	Name and Address	Telephone	Director and Assistant Director
STATE COORDINATOR	Department of Health and Social Services Madison 53701	266-1511	Jack Borders, Safety Consultant
Eau Claire	Poison Control Center Luther Hospital 310 Chestnut St. 54701	832-6611 Ext. 227	Paul G. Bjerke, R. Ph.
Green Bay	Poison Information Center Bellin Memorial Hospital 744 S. Webster Ave. 54301	437-9031 Ext. 257	S. L. Griggs, M.D. Mrs. M. L. Neetzel, R.N.
Kenosha	Poison Control Center Kenosha Hospital 6308 8th Ave. 53140	656-2201	Dorothy Conzelman, M.D. Mrs. Emily Haubrick, R.N.
Madison	Poison Information Center University Hospital Department of Pharmacology 1300 University Ave. 53706	262-3702	David Zilz, R. Ph. Monte Cohon, R. Ph.
Milwaukee	Poison Control Center Milwaukee Children's Hospital 1700 W. Wisconsin 53233	344-7100 Ext. 308	John C. Peterson, M.D. Elaine Kohler, M.D.

WYOMING

STATE COORDINATOR	State Department of Public Health Cheyenne 82001	777-7275	H. S. Parish, M.D., Director, Division of Preventive Medicine
Casper	Poison Control Center Natrona County Hospital 1233 E. 2nd St. 82601	235-1311 Ext. 131	D. L. Becker, M.D. Jay J. Smith, R. Ph.
Cheyenne	Poison Control Center Laramie County Memorial Hospital 23rd & House Sts. 82001	634-3341 Ext. 238	Lawrence J. Cohen, M.D. Rachel Garlick, R.N.

Index

Important Telephone Numbers

Fill in this page now and keep it near your telephone so
that it will be available in case of an emergency. Other
members of your family—and your baby-sitter—also
should know where it is.

EMERGENCY NUMBERS

NAME   **NUMBER**

Your Child's Doctor_____

   (Pediatrician)_____

Alternate Doctor_____

Family Doctor_____

Hospital_____

Neighbor to Help in Emergency _____

Police_____

Fire Department _____

Ambulance_____

Poison Control Center_____

OTHER IMPORTANT NUMBERS

Pharmacy_____

All-Night Pharmacy_____

Husband at Work _____

Mother_____

Mother-in-Law_____

Clergyman_____

Baby-Sitter_____

Nurse or Nursing Service_____

Diaper Service_____

Plumber_____

Electrician_____

Appliance Serviceman_____